CM
MS

D0891727

EUROPEAN UNION DEVELOPMENT POLICY

Also by Marjorie Lister

THE EUROPEAN COMMUNITY AND THE DEVELOPING WORLD
THE EUROPEAN UNION AND THE SOUTH

European Union Development Policy

Edited by

Marjorie Lister
Lecturer in European-Developing Country Relations
Department of European Studies
University of Bradford

338.9114
E89

First published in Great Britain 1998 by
MACMILLAN PRESS LTD
Houndmills, Basingstoke, Hampshire RG21 6XS and London
Companies and representatives throughout the world

A catalogue record for this book is available from the British Library.

ISBN 0–333–71656–6

First published in the United States of America 1998 by
ST. MARTIN'S PRESS, INC.,
Scholarly and Reference Division,
175 Fifth Avenue, New York, N.Y. 10010

ISBN 0–312–21538–X

Library of Congress Cataloging-in-Publication Data
European Union development policy / edited by Marjorie Lister.
p.   cm.
"Based on the 'Europe and the Developing Countries Conference'
held ... in London in late 1996."
Includes bibliographical references and index.
ISBN 0–312–21538–X
1. Economic assistance, European—Congresses.   2. Developing
countries—Economic conditions—Congresses.   3. European Union
countries—Foreign economic relations—Developing countries-
-Congresses.   4. Developing countries—Foreign economic relations-
-European Union countries—Congresses.   I. Lister, Marjorie, 1955–

HC60.E7965   1998
338.91'14—dc21   98–14873
                                                                          CIP

This book is printed on paper suitable for recycling and made from fully managed and
sustained forest sources.

10   9   8   7   6   5   4   3   2   1
07   06   05   04   03   02   01   00   99   98

Printed and bound in Great Britain by
Antony Rowe Ltd, Chippenham, Wiltshire

Contents

v

Acknowledgements

The editor wishes to thank Ms Margaret Haldane, Postgraduate Secretary of the Department of European Studies, and Mrs Grace Hudson, of the J B Priestley Library, Bradford University, for their help in the preparation of this book.

List of Abbreviations

ACP	African, Caribbean and Pacific States
APEC	Asia-Pacific Economic Cooperation (group of states)
CAP	Common Agricultural Policy
DOM/TOM	France's overseas departments and overseas territories
DAC	Development Assistance Committee
DOM/TOM	Département d'outre mer; Territoire d'outre mer
EDF	European Development Fund
EU	European Union
FCO	Foreign and Commonwealth Office (UK)
FTA	Free Trade Area
IBRD	International Bank for Reconstruction and Development (World Bank)
ICO	International Coffee Organisation
LDC	Less developed country
LLDC	Least developed country
NGO	Non-governmental organisation
NIP	National Indicative Programme
ODA	Official Development Assistance; also Overseas Development Administration (UK)
OECD	Organisation for Economic Cooperation and Development
PMDT	Processing, marketing, distribution and transport
UNDP	United Nations Development Programme
PNG	Papua New Guinea
SACU	Southern African Customs Union
SADC	Southern African Development Community
WTO	World Trade Organisation

Notes on the Contributors

Lynda Chalker (Baroness Chalker of Wallasey) was a member of the UK Parliament from 1974 to 1992. Lady Chalker was a government minister for 18 years, becoming Minister for Overseas Development in 1989. She was created a Life Peer in 1992. Following her retirement from government in 1997, Baroness Chalker has been working as an independent consultant on projects in central and southern Africa.

Gordon Crawford is Lecturer in Development Studies, Centre for Development Studies, School of International, Development and European Studies in the University of Leeds. His interests are in the politics and sociology of development, particularly the realisation of human rights, North and South. Mr Crawford's recent research has focused on political conditionality and the promotion of human rights and democracy through development assistance.

Carl B. Greenidge, a well-known Caribbean personality and currently Deputy Secretary-General of the African, Caribbean and Pacific Group of States, has worked as a professional economist in Europe, Africa and the Caribbean. As Guyana's Minister of Finance from 1983 to 1992, he was President of the ACP–EU Council of Ministers when the Lomé IV negotiations opened. Previously Mr Greenidge was ACP Ministerial Spokesman on Sugar as well as ACP Negotiator on Trade (Lomé III).

Friedrich Hamburger was born in Vienna, Austria, and studied law and political science. He worked for 25 years in the Austrian Foreign Service, attaining the rank of Ambassador as the Chief of the Cabinet of the Austrian Vice-Chancellor. Since November 1995 Dr Hamburger has been Director for Development Policy in the European Commission.

Adrian Hewitt is Deputy Director of the Overseas Development Institute (ODI), manages the ODI fellowship scheme and is the Research Adviser to the All-Party Parliamentary Group on Overseas Development in the UK Parliament. His current research work covers the trade and aid policies of the European Union. Mr Hewitt is a co-editor of the *Development Policy Review* and an editorial board member of *Third World Quarterly*.

Michael Hindley is a graduate of London University in German Studies and of Lancaster University (MA) in Comparative Cultural Studies. He has been a member of the European Parliament since 1984 and is co-ordinator of the Socialist Group on Trade Policies. Mr Hindley specialises in the external relations of the EU and in issues of human and social rights conditionality in world trade.

Marjorie Lister is Lecturer in European–Developing Country Relations at the University of Bradford. She is the author of many articles and two books on the subject of the European Union's policies towards developing countries. Most recently, Dr Lister has published *The European Union and the South* (1997).

Simon Maxwell Director of the Overseas Development Institute in London, and was formerly a Fellow of the Institute of Development Studies at the University of Sussex, and Programme Manager for Poverty, Food Security and the Environment. He is an economist who has written widely on food security, poverty and aid.

Gorm Rye Olsen is Senior Lecturer at the Centre of African Studies, University of Copenhagen, while he is on leave from his post as senior research fellow at the Center for Development Research, Copenhagen. Dr Olsen's current research project is entitled, 'Europe's relationship to sub-Saharan Africa in the post-cold war era with special reference to aid'.

Charles Henry Plumb (Baron Plumb of Coleshill) has been a member of the European Parliament since 1979. He has held many distinguished posts including President of the National Farmers' Union of England and Wales, President of the European Parliament, Leader of the British Conservatives in the European Parliament, and Co-Chairman of the ACP–EU Joint Assembly.

Introduction

Marjorie Lister

The current state of the relations between North and South can be broadly defined by reference to a number of keywords: liberalisation (of markets), globalisation (of the world economy), fragmentation (of the old Cold War blocs), and the marginalisation of the poorest countries.[1] In the context of the relations of the fifteen-member European Union (EU) and the developing world, the contemporary impasse of development theory and practice can be seen as undermining the best efforts of the EU and its developing partners to create a new relationship in the twenty-first century.[2]

EU Commission Vice-President Marin argued that after the fall of the Berlin Wall in 1989, the EU suddenly woke up to the significance of its external relations: 'the EU only recently realised the importance of its external relations and, for the first time, it defined two clear strategic priorities: Central and Eastern European and the Mediterranean region'.[3] It is true that in the 1990s the EU's priorities have changed, but what Commissioner Marin calls the 'unprecedented habit of dialogue' of the EU and the Mediterranean countries since the Barcelona Conference of 1995 was preceded by a similar habit of dialogue with the developing countries of Africa, the Caribbean and Pacific.[4]

The European Union conceives of its development policy in terms both of opportunities and responsibilities. The opportunities include managing 'global interdependence and risks, and the promotion of a kind of world development that is more compatible with European political and social values'. Moreover, development policy in the next century could be for Europe 'a gateway to regions with enormous development potential which are now starting to bestir themselves'.[5] In its relations with the countries of the southern Mediterranean littoral, with Latin America and Asia, Europe could well find profitable trade and investment opportunities.

It is in terms of its responsibilities that the EU finds more problems. How can it find a 'new footing' for its long-standing relationship with the (now) 71 African, Caribbean and Pacific (ACP) countries? How can poverty, inequality and human misery be reduced using the same tools of development which have so far failed to achieve this? The 1992 Treaty on European Union (Treaty of Maastricht) set out the goals of development cooperation: the sustainable economic and social development of the developing countries, especially the poorest; the integration of the

developing countries into the world economy; the campaign against poverty; support for democracy, human rights and the rule of law.[6] But despite
having these objectives, as 'social forces' theory observes, it is less the
legalistic statements which render these objectives operational than the
underlying environment and commitment to them, and the ways in
which they are implemented.

It is in these latter areas that EU cooperation with Africa, the Caribbean and Pacific can be called into question. The European Commission
itself has recognised that this partnership has lost its substance, but this is
not solely the fault of the ACP, but also of EU drift. When the EU invites
the ACP to enter a dialogue that is 'part and parcel of its common foreign policy'[7] it should be recalled that the nature of the EU itself is un-
clear, and its foreign policy has not been very coherent or successful in
areas such as former Yugoslavia, Albania or Zaire.[8]

Any verdict now on the results of European Union development policy, and the Lomé policy in particular, could be premature. In a similar
way, an observer of the EU during its period of 'eurosclerosis' in the
1980s would have been unable to predict the current rapid development
of European integration, including the prospect of economic and monetary integration. The four decades of EEC/EU cooperation with the
ACP and other developing countries up to now may have done no more
than lay the foundations for the expansion and development of relations
in the future.

This book addresses the issue of the European Union's development
policy in a variety of ways. It is based on the 'Europe and the Developing
Countries Conference' held in the European Parliament office in London in late 1996, which brought together both political practitioners and
academic observers of European development policy for a wide-ranging
debate on its present status and future prospects. The expiration of the
Lomé IV Convention in February 2000, and the necessity of either re-
placing, reordering or abandoning the Lomé system, was an underlying
theme of several contributors. This text is divided into two sections: the
first comprises short contributions from active politicians and a senior
European civil servant. These give a good account of current debates
within the UK's development ministry, the European Parliament and
Commission. The second section includes longer papers from the ACP
Deputy Secretary-General and an international group of academics and
development specialists.

In the first section the UK's Minister for Overseas Development, Baroness Chalker, balances the sometimes-negative image of EU aid with
references to its successes and – even more – its challenges. She argues

that the growth of European aid, its new emphasis on the Mediterranean countries and its internal organization constitute challenges for the future. Keeping the poverty focus of EU development cooperation while improving aid coordination and delivery are among the complex issues to which no one yet has all the answers. The UK, however, wants to play a central role in the debate.

In his contribution on fair trade, Michael Hindley, Vice-President of the External Affairs Committee of the European Parliament, focuses on the disadvantages small nations face in the world economy. He describes how St Lucia and St Vincent had considerable difficulty in defending their vital interest in the EU's banana-trading regime. Whether in negotiations with the World Trade Organisation, the USA or the EU, small states face a big gap between their technical expertise and that of the developed world.

Lord Plumb, leader of the Conservatives in the European Parliament, looks at the European context of development. He stresses the importance of reviewing the whole of European development policies and not just reacting to certain criticisms. He argues that parity is the essence of the Joint ACP–EU Assembly and likewise, the ACP input into discussions about the future of development policy is essential. Lord Plumb sees an important role for private investment, non-governmental organisations and the good governance and human rights agendas in fostering development. The reduction of EU development aid to areas outside the Mediterranean is a distressing development, and one which the European Parliament and the Joint ACP–EU Assembly are vigorously campaigning against.

Friedrich Hamburger, Director for Development Policy in the European Commission, acknowledges the increasing diversity of the EU's external interests, but argues that relations with the ACP countries remain 'the cornerstone' of European development policy. Compared to other developed countries, the EU is a relatively generous aid donor, but it needs to strengthen the coherence, partnership, and poverty focus of its development policy. The EU should improve its aid conditionality, work towards two-way free trade with developing countries and take on a role of global leadership. The many changes occurring at the end of this century should give rise not to despondency, but to a new sense of purpose and commitment.

In the second section, Chapter 5 examines changes in the relative priorities accorded to different developing regions by the European Union. The present impasse of development theory and the failure of the international development system so far effectively to deliver development suggest that the time is not right for bold new initiatives such as unmaking the Lomé Convention. Instead, building on an inchoate yet longstanding European goodwill towards the process of development, the EU should concentrate on improving the 'acquis Lomé'. The themes of regionalism versus globalism and the analysis of the Lomé Convention as an international regime lead to the conclusion that the cause of a forthcoming 'development century' is best served by not putting an untimely end to EU–ACP cooperation.

The Deputy Secretary-General of the ACP Group, Carl B. Greenidge, poses the question in Chapter 6 of whether the ACP Group has common characteristics in terms of its commodity dependence and market concentration. He examines the parlous economic conditions of many ACP countries but also finds cases of sound policies and positive economic growth. Falling levels of aid and Europe's reluctance to discuss debt issues are disheartening. Declining commodity prices, problems of market access and low levels of preferences mean that trade has not been an 'engine of growth' for the ACP countries as a group, but some have increased their exports rapidly in recent years. Foreign direct investment to Africa is low and stagnating. The EU could help the ACP both to gain better tariff treatment for the least developed countries and to attract more foreign investment.

Partnership is a strongly entrenched aspect of successive Lomé Conventions. It is perhaps most significant in terms of the operation of the joint Lomé institutions. The ACP countries need to fashion policies to address the inconsistencies in EU attitudes and practices in the areas of human rights, good governance and democracy. Changes in the Lomé relationship will be needed, but they may not have to be as radical as is frequently claimed.

In Chapter 7, Gorm Rye Olsen analyses the determinants of European policy-making which could keep Africa on the political and developmental agenda. He focuses on three major aid donors: Germany, Denmark and the UK. Since aid is primarily derived from donors' interests and policies, assessing them provides important insights into the future of European development policies. In the case of Germany, weak aid and pro-Africa lobbies, combined with divided policy-making organisations, mean that aid levels could be in jeopardy if German economic interests seem threatened.

Denmark, by contrast, is characterised by a 'remarkable unanimity of actors in policy-making'. Denmark's priorities in development are poverty reduction and Africa. The aid ministry, Danida, is well organised and central to policy-making. Denmark's broad foreign policy interests are served by its commitment to aid and humane internationalism.

For the UK, the situation is very different: less harmonious and more complex. Commercial interests have a higher priority; the UK also acts as a 'power broker', organising international coalitions and preserving the Commonwealth. Civil servants and the aid minister work within a relatively weak department whose role may be only to resist decline. The chances of keeping aid to Africa on the UK policy agenda therefore seem very small. For each of the three countries studied, bureaucratic interests in aid ministries and non-governmental organisations (NGOs) form the most important determinants of aid policy. By extension, this is also likely to be true for other bilateral European aid (except France) and for European Union aid programmes.

In a chapter analysing the case of Ethiopia, Simon Maxwell, Director of the Overseas Development Institute, outlines the 'maximalist', and 'minimalist' approaches to the future of European development aid. The maximalists favour increasing the power and influence of European development policy, even to the point where national aid policies wither away. Minimalists, by contrast, want to 're-nationalise' aid. Among the factors deciding this debate, the quality of EU aid is of central importance. As one of the authors of the first full-scale study of EU aid to one country, Ethiopia, Simon Maxwell explains the methodological complexity of posing the question: Does European aid work? He concludes that some – even most – of the aid did work and proposes a seven-point strategy further to improve its results. Simplifying procedures, decentralising and delegating authority to the field are of crucial importance in improving aid administration.

In Chapter 9, Adrian Hewitt assesses the changes in UK and EU aid policies to the Pacific region. Africa may have been the essence of the African, Caribbean and Pacific Group of States, but the Pacific states do matter. However, in order to reduce its total aid budget, and concentrate a larger share of aid on fewer countries, the UK is sharply cutting its assistance to the Pacific region. In effect the UK is transferring its involvement to the EU. However, it is not proven that EU aid is better than UK aid in terms of value for money; neither were the Pacific states consulted over the changes. Europe's growing interest in regions such as Eastern Europe and the former USSR, and the reluctance of other bilateral and multilateral donors to focus on the Pacific, mean the region could face marginalisation. Even Australia has cut aid to its Pacific neighbours.

Richer than most of sub-Saharan Africa, yet poorer than most of the Caribbean, the Pacific ACP countries still need Europe's assistance. As part of a growing region where the Europeans could usefully have more links, not fewer, the Pacific ACP states offer the UK and EU opportunities for cooperation they should not throw away.

The issue of promoting human rights and democracy is one of the most controversial areas in EU development policy. Not only the EU, but also the USA and the major international organizations are grappling with the complexities of this issue.[9] Gordon Crawford assesses the inclusion of human rights and democracy clauses in development agreements and the use of sanctions when these are transgressed. He sets a high standard of moving 'towards policy being applied in an objective, non-selective, fair and equal manner'. In practice, Gordon Crawford finds that sanctions have been much more stringently imposed on sub-Saharan Africa than on other regions. Moreover, the severity of the sanctions imposed does not correspond to the degree of violation of the principles of human rights and democracy.

Several EU members are unwilling to restrict their arms sales in accordance with their human rights policy. Economic and political considerations, some left over from the Cold War, have led to a selective and inconsistent application of human rights principles. Crawford argues for a fully-defined, universal code of political and civil rights. This code should then be implemented fairly in a transparent, strictly monitored, and internationalised process.

In summary, the themes running through this book are themes of change and challenge: how to respond to the need for change to mark the end of the millennium; how to respond to the globalised markets and the end of the Cold War; how to build partnerships in regions newly deemed important; whether and how to reorganise old relationships that have faltered; how to improve aid effectiveness; how to promote human rights and good governance in developing countries. So far, the inputs of developing countries into these debates have been of secondary importance. Europe has had trouble, for instance, in hearing the statements from ACP leaders that they regard their Group as still viable and effective.[10]

On one hand, EU development policy in the late 1990s lives in an environment of 'Eurafropessimism'. The EU lacks confidence in its ability to sustain and to create new partnerships with developing countries or to achieve development objectives. The Union calls for intensified partnership and dialogue with the South, but when a developing country like South Africa expresses diverging views, the EU finds it extremely difficult to cope with these.[11]

On the other hand, the European Union and its member states clearly understand many of the problems of administration, complementarity and coherence of EU development policy. And if they understand these problems, the EU can take action to rectify them. The end of the millennium is a convenient marker, but it does not necessarily have to coincide with re-starting EU development policies 'from scratch'.[12] In its recent Green Paper on relations with the ACP countries, the Union expresses idealistic objectives very similar to those set out 40 years ago in the Treaty of Rome. Only Europe's crisis of confidence can prevent it from making progress in achieving them: 'What we make of the post-Lomé world is essentially a political choice and the future partnership must meet the new concerns of Europeans and live up to the expectations of the ACP peoples.'[13]

MARJORIE LISTER

Notes

1. European Commission, 'Green Paper on relations between the European Union and the ACP countries on the eve of the 21st century: challenges and options for a new partnership', Directorate-General VIII Development, Brussels, 20 November 1996, p. i.
2. Adams, Nassau, *Worlds Apart: the North–South Divide and the International System*, Zed Books, London and New Jersey, 1993, p. 248, takes a hopeful view of the present stalemate: 'the current impasse in North–South relations, and the seemingly inexorable process by which these two poles of humanity are drifting economically apart. If nothing else, they serve to remind us that, unyielding as current trends may seem, they may themselves contain the seeds of change'.
3. Marin, Commissioner Manuel, 'The European Union's Mediterranean Policy', speech to the Royal Institute of International Affairs, London, 6 March 1997, p. 2.
4. Marin, *ibid.*, p. 10.
5. European Commission, 'Green Paper', p. iv.
6. *The Unseen Treaty: Treaty on European Union, Maastricht 1992*, Oxford, Folly Bridge Workshops, 1992, Title XVII, Article 130u.
7. European Commission, 'Green Paper', p. vi.
8. Former EU Commission President Jacques Delors called the EU 'an unidentified political object'. Delors, Jacques, 'I cannot resign myself to this decline of Europe' The *Independent*, 24 October 1996.
9. For a discussion of the near-inescapable double standards involved in implementing human rights, see Neier, Aryeh, 'The New Double Standard' and Garten, Jeffrey, 'Comment: the Need for Pragmatism', *Foreign Policy*, No. 105, Winter 1996–7. For the argument that human rights are culturally determined, not universal, see Bozeman, Adda, 'How to Think about Human Rights', *Proceedings of the National Security Affairs Conference – 1977*,

National Defense University, Washington, D.C, 18–20 July 1977; also *Strategic Intelligence and Statecraft*, Brassey's, Washington, New York, London, 1992. In 'Implementing the Right to Development? Analysis of European Community Development and Human Rights Policies', *Human Rights in Developing Countries Yearbook 1996*, The Hague, Kluwer Law Publications, 1996, Karin Arts observes that the EU has had trouble coming to terms with the UN's right to development.

10. Cumberbatch, Ambassador Lingston, 'Are Globalisation and Development Mutually Exclusive?', *Beyond Lomé IV: Exploring Options for Future ACP–EU Cooperation*, Policy Management Report No. 6, European Centre for Development Policy Management, October 1996, pp. 70–1.

11. Southey, Caroline, 'EU's patience is running out', *Financial Times*, 25 March 1997, 'Survey: Investing in South Africa', p. 3.

12. European Commission, 'Green Paper', p. 6.

13. European Commission, 'Green Paper', p. III.

1 The UK's View of the Future of European Development Cooperation

Baroness Chalker of Wallasey

F35   079

I want to start today by setting aside some myths. We have all too often seen EC development programmes as monolithic, as bureaucratic, as a threat to what we do best – our bilateral assistance. All negative images.

Of course there are challenges for EC development assistance – real ones. But there are also successes – and real opportunities. Most of all we must recognise that EC programmes are *our* programmes, and we must be part of the debate about the present and the future. We must face the challenges, just as we must share the credit for the successes.

I want to look today at some current issues, as well as the future. Firstly, let's look at how EC external assistance has changed, and what that means for us.

For a start, it has grown dramatically. When I took over as Minister for Overseas Development in 1989 the total Community expenditure on external assistance was 2.3 billion ecu. The expenditure for 1996 is expected to be 5.5 billion ecu – almost two and a half times as much – and that means two and a half times more out of my budget. That's not easy for me.

Its geographical spread has also changed. In 1989, 94 per cent of EC assistance went to the more traditional recipients – sub-Saharan Africa, the Caribbean, the Pacific, Asia, Latin America – leaving just 6 per cent for other recipients. In 1996 these other recipients – mainly the countries of central Asia, eastern Europe, and the Mediterranean – will receive around half of the EC's external assistance. That's another challenge for a country like Britain which believes in focusing development assistance on the poorest.

More positively, we have seen real success – for example, through the increasingly central role which the Commission has played in the process of economic reform in Africa. I applaud this. We have also seen much greater cooperation between the Commission and Member States across the board in recent years. Under the last UK Presidency, we initiated Horizon 2000 – an agenda to develop common EU policy guidelines

1

on development cooperation. And we have seen substantial progress on areas including poverty, health, HIV/AIDS, food security, education and gender. These all apply to both member states and the Commission – a coordinated approach.

But Horizon 2000 is also about *operational* coordination; and we are working hard to make a success of the pilot coordination exercises in six countries. It's a slow process; but one which we cannot afford to let fail. Our core task is not to agree policy guidelines in Brussels. It is to make sure that our assistance makes a real difference to the poor.

That is why it is so important to get the *management* of development assistance right. It's not an easy job, but it must be tackled.

This year's excellent DAC report on EC development assistance is a good starting point. It highlighted the difficulties linked to the present complex organisational structure – five Commissioners are responsible for external assistance through four Directorates General as well as through the European Community Humanitarian Office (ECHO). We need to see streamlining in the structure, and we need better linkages between different parts of the Commission. I know this means treading on toes. I know it means interfering with closely monitored boundaries. But I also know that without it we shall never achieve the efficiency and effectiveness which the developing world needs.

This is not just a question of reorganisation. It's also about filling skills gaps in basic areas such as poverty alleviation, gender and the environment; it's about further application of the 'project cycle management' methodology; and about the proper use of evaluation results in new project design.

But this Conference is not just about looking at the present. It's also about looking at the future. There are big and complicated issues to address. The fourth Lomé Convention, which governs relations with the African, Caribbean and Pacific countries, runs out at the end of the decade. The Edinburgh Perspectives, which form the ceiling for budget spending under which all other EC external assistance is given, run out around the same time. So big decisions are needed on *all* EC external assistance. Work has already started – the Commission is soon to produce its own Green Paper about the post-Lomé arrangements. We have a long way to go, and a good deal of thinking to do. But I am clear about some of the key principles. First and foremost, I want to see development assistance focused on the poorest. I want to re-assert their centrality to EU development policy. This is an approach which the UK has advocated for many years and I was delighted that the G7 countries adopted it at Lyon in June.

My second principle is that assistance must also be concentrated on those needy countries that can *use it effectively* – another principle now agreed by the G7. We owe this to our taxpayers. We also owe it to those recipients who are undertaking tough economic, social and political reforms. The EU, both collectively and through the Commission, is too big a donor to be sending mixed messages about reform.

So we need to think about a range of issues – but finding the right framework and the right global allocation of EC development assistance resources will be two of the most important.

On the framework – the architecture – we need to consider whether it makes sense to keep the ACP grouping for the next century. Would it for instance be possible to increase the poverty focus by including poor countries of Asia in the group? Or perhaps the grouping should be split up into smaller regional blocks? I still have an open mind. Whatever options are considered, the final choice must be guided by the principle of allocation according to need and ability to use development assistance effectively. We also need to look at the terms of our assistance. Grant funding must be right for the poorest. But there may be a case for providing more of our assistance to middle-income countries in the form of loans, whilst focusing our grant assistance on the poorest.

So far, I have spoken only about development assistance. Of course this is vital for those who need it. But for all developing countries, trade is even more important – in 1994 total developing country export earnings were eight times as great as their receipts from development assistance. In this area of trade we should also have a new look at the way Europe responds to developing country needs.

A lot has happened since the Lomé trade preferences were first designed. We need to take account of new developments in international trade. General liberalisation will erode past preferential margins. New arrangements will have to be compatible with the rules of the WTO.

We must all embrace this new era of freer global trade. We have already set out our vision of free trade for all by 2020. This will allow developing countries – ACP and others alike – to exploit their comparative advantages.

In the meantime, we welcome the proposal by the Director General of the WTO that all richer countries should allow the least developed countries guaranteed tariff-free access to their markets. This will help to bring these countries more fully into the world trading system. We will be pressing others within the Union and beyond to join us in supporting this idea. Even this proposal will eventually be overtaken, as we move towards the free-trade regime which is in all our interests, EU and developing countries alike. But in the medium term it is an important initiative to help the poorest countries.

I started out by talking about challenges and opportunities. In a business as complex as development, no one has all the answers. What I want to see is a real debate about the issues. I want to see the UK playing a central role in that debate.

2 Fair Trade Needs Fair Access to Court

Michael Hindley

The decision not to allow lawyers representing Lucia and St Vincent to attend a World Trade Organisation (WTO) disputes panel on the highly complex issue of the European Union's (EU) banana regime raises alarming questions about the usefulness and accessibility, particularly to smaller nations, of the WTO itself. The actual dispute hinges on the fact that the EU through its Afro–Caribbean–Pacific (ACP) programme practices positive discrimination in favour of small-island banana production in the Caribbean. This certainly helps the smaller, often family producers in the mainly former British colonies. They can maintain market share in the face of tough competition from plantation production by largely American multinationals in Central America – the so-called 'Dollar Bananas'.

There is not a united front in the EU either; the Germans have challenged the EU's discrimination on the grounds that German (and other EU) consumers should have access to the longer – and if the concessions to other bananas are stopped – cheaper dollar bananas. The EU's favouritism has been challenged at the WTO by the USA, Guatemala, Mexico and Honduras.

The WTO has set up a disputes panel to take evidence to help it make a judgement. The establishment of this strengthened disputes mechanism was generally greeted favourably by developing countries because it institutionalises 'rules-based trade'. Binding decisions enforced on the great as well as the small was seen as an improvement on the old GATT disputes system whose rulings could be ignored with impunity, and were, by the large trade players.

Access to the WTO is rightly in my view by governments only. This means that anyone with a grievance has to convince a government to proceed with its case. Some non-governmental organisations (NGOs) are pressing for their own direct access and so too are some large multinational traders and some lawyers. As access to any of these bodies is impossible to grant without access to the others, in my view access for none is preferable. If lawyers are allowed direct access, it will mean that trade law, like the civil law in many countries, will become the preserve of those who can afford it rather than those who need it.

However, just how accessible to developing countries the WTO is, is clearly thrown into doubt by the panel decision to accept the objections of the governments of the USA and others, to St Lucia and St Vincent being represented by a private law firm. St Lucia and smaller countries have at the moment no option but to hire expertise. The reality is that smaller countries cannot even maintain diplomatic missions to the United Nations (UN) in Geneva. But large governments are well represented at the WTO and other UN bodies like UNCTAD and UNHCR. Smaller countries simply cannot afford the staff to take up the representation they are entitled to and therefore will be at a distinct disadvantage in any dispute with a large country. The USA and the EU, the dominant trading entities, have sufficient in-house legal expertise on the Trade Department and Trade Directorate payrolls.

Setting up a 'rules-based' trading system was one of the selling points to encourage developing countries to sign the final GATT settlement. That the GATT was a 'rich men's club' was a widespread and accurate criticism. If legal aid for smaller countries is excluded on a technicality, the WTO risks being labelled the same. Indeed, the final GATT settlement stated: 'Ministers recognise the need for strengthening the capability of the GATT and the WTO to provide increased technical assistance in their areas of competence, in particular, to substantially expand its provisions to the least developed countries'. This explicit recognition of the need for technical aid from the developed traders to the less developed traders needs to be put into practice.

Certainly, the EU has the capacity within its bilateral aid packages with third countries to provide such technical assistance. Individual member states have a similar capacity. Trade is not simply about moving goods around, and 'fair trade' should be more than a slogan. Clearly it is in everyone's interest to have non-partisan judgements on trade disputes, and those decisions will form the custom-and-practice for future trading relations.

There is little point encouraging the world to trade if the technical wherewithal is not provided to allow all to trade on a fair basis. In the meantime, though, latitude must be given to the smaller countries. It is already accepted in other areas of international law that outsiders may help not only to prepare but also to present cases.

The Vienna Convention on the Law of Treaties provides that representatives accredited by states to an international conference or to an international organisation, or one of its organs, are considered as representing that state. It is vital that the WTO is brought swiftly into line with the norms of international behaviour.

Postscript

There is an encouraging conclusion to this story which underlines the benefit of political pressure. Shortly after delivering this paper, I was informed by an EC Commission official that the Commission had used its good offices with the WTO to intervene on behalf of St Lucia and St Vincent to enable their representatives to be readmitted to the disputes panel. I and other MEPs had asked the Commission to do so in the course of exchanges in the External Economic Affairs Committee and I was both grateful and gratified that the Commission heeded our request.

However, the general point of access holds good. Developing countries should be allowed the same degree of flexibility in their representations to the WTO as other international bodies allow as a matter of course and of right, and not thanks to the benign and welcome intervention of the EU.

3 The Lomé Convention, Human Rights and Europe
Lord Plumb

J24 F13 $\frac{o15}{o19}$ $\bar{o}^{10}$

This is a subject which is very important to me, but more to the point is important for millions of people from all over the developing world. The countdown has begun. Lomé IV runs out on the 29th of February 2000. The mid-term review and financial protocol for the second term was completed in Mauritania almost a year late.

Negotiations will begin to examine what conditions will subsequently govern relations between the EU and Member States on the one hand, and ACP States on the other. In the recent Joint Assembly in Luxembourg there was unanimous agreement that the Convention needs to be thoroughly reviewed in the new international context and in light of EU developments.

It is imperative that ACP partners play an active part in the thought process concerning future relations and we must avoid any unnecessary panic among member countries. Lomé has been the framework for co-operation since 1975 and in many respects has acted as a pilot scheme for other forms of cooperation.

As we approach 2000, it is essential that we shape the whole of the EU's development policy rather than just react to a certain fashion that seeks to portray Lomé as a post-colonial anachronism.

The text of the Maastricht Treaty specifies the way ahead quite clearly – development policy should promote sustainable development, particularly in the most disadvantaged countries, the fight against poverty in developing countries, and the smooth and gradual integration of developing countries in the world economy.

No one expects miracles, but the obvious step is to make developing countries more competitive with a fair chance for trade in a world market. Our underlying aim is to assist the African, Caribbean and Pacific countries to enhance the well-being of their peoples. It is not for the Europeans to decide how this can best be achieved. Joint action on proposals from the ACP must be the basis of our reflections. Hence the role of the Joint Assembly: an organ of which the very essence is parity.

At the same time, certain fundamental principles stand out. As populations in the South increase, and as expectations very correctly and naturally grow, it is necessary to find ways of developing economic and social growth and of creating jobs, through the encouragement of self-help. Without investment this cannot be realised. It is our task to help the ACP countries to create a favourable investment climate so that private and public funds can flow into the African, Caribbean and Pacific regions.

It is my conviction that private investment can be attracted to the ACP countries. These countries are rich in natural resources and, in most cases, manpower is abundant. What need to be built up are the economic and legal climate for investment, and the skills of the workforce. The European Union can help the ACP States in the creation of a favourable economic and legal climate, but the ultimate responsibility will always remain with the countries themselves. Only they can ensure good governance.

The Lomé Convention already devotes important resources to manpower training. Even greater attention must be paid to appropriate academic and particularly technical education. In this respect it would be difficult to over-emphasise the role of the non-governmental organisations (NGOs). In all aspects of our development policies the NGOs fulfil an invaluable function, but most particularly in education and in health.

We agreed in our recent assembly proposals to accord observer status to NGO networks from both the European Union and the South. Without their cooperation our work would be much less fruitful. I have no doubt that the presence of NGOs as observers will enrich our deliberations. The NGOs, and particularly the southern NGOs, know precisely what the situation is on the ground. For this reason it is always beneficial to consult with NGOs and to give due weight to their assessments.

Growing populations need increased food supplies. Urban growth, the subject of one of our Joint Assembly working groups, further enhances the need for higher yields in the countryside. The more people that live in towns, the more the rural areas have to produce food. The main thrust of the Third Lomé Convention was the enhancement of food self-sufficiency and the encouragement of rural development. This emphasis has been continued in the Fourth Lomé Convention, and will become all the more important in the twenty-first century. The successor arrangement to Lomé IV must address the issue of increasing ACP food production, while respecting the environment.

The situation in the Great Lakes region of Africa, and also in Nigeria, Liberia, Somalia and Sudan is extremely delicate. The tensions giving rise to crises are so often due to lack of tolerance for ethnic and religious differences, and failure to respect human rights. The mid-term revision of Lomé IV, when it comes into force, will further strengthen our joint commitment to respect human rights.

Human rights are at the heart of our preoccupations. As our aim is to improve the well-being of all the people in all our 85 countries, and as that well-being implies fair treatment, it is right that such importance be accorded to human rights and human dignity. Concepts of human rights can certainly vary from culture to culture, and there must be flexibility with regard to details. However, certain fundamentals remain essential, as laid down in the UN Charter on Human Rights and the African Charter on Human and Peoples' Rights. If the Joint Assembly were to accept lower human rights standards from certain countries than from others, that would constitute not only a form of discrimination but, even worse, lack of respect. We would in fact be saying 'there is one rule for Europe, and another rule for the ACP'. Such a patronising attitude is quite unacceptable. We care about how our citizens are treated, no matter in which signatory state of the Convention they may happen to live. We condemn human rights abuses wherever they are brought to our attention, be it in Europe or in an ACP country. This is a manifestation of our respect for the dignity of all men and women wherever they live. It is because of our belief in the fundamental *equality* and *humanity* of all our people that we emphasise human rights, and devote so much of our time to human rights issues.

The proposals for the 1997 budget of the European Union show a distressing reduction in the funds allocated to the developing countries outside the Mediterranean region. Those of us in the European Parliament involved in development cooperation are campaigning vigorously against such cuts, which run counter to our traditional development policies. I am afraid that it will not be easy to influence European public opinion. One of the roles of the Joint Assembly must be to ensure that the people of Europe have confidence in the progress being made by the countries of the South. We must all help in this task of confidence-building. Africa in particular has had a bad press in recent years. Many people with only a superficial interest in international affairs see Africa only as a continent of unrest and civil wars. There is insufficient awareness of the enormous progress being made with respect to democratisation and constitutional stability. So many Europeans do not realise that a number of African countries are enjoying encouraging economic growth, and that in an even larger number of countries, governments are being appointed democratically through multi-party electoral processes. The good news is not mentioned, even on the inside pages. The bad news makes front-page headlines.

Institutional reform has led to a heartening growth in the number of democratic regimes. While in some cases democracy is flawed and parties or even leaders are associated with one ethnic group, nevertheless democratisation and good government are making progress. One must remember that European democracy took centuries to evolve. A perfect democratic system cannot emerge in Africa in the space of a few years. Each country and region has to evolve its own system, although this must be based on certain universal principles of human rights.

In conclusion, EU aid is not merely economic. It encompasses EU assistance to areas such as environment, health, AIDS, demography and population, drug abuse and social problems. Some of its policies help to reduce immigration flows from the South to the EU. This is particularly true of the aid to the southern Mediterranean countries. It could be said that assistance now will reduce the migration pressures in the future which could have enormous human and financial costs for the EU and its Member States.

EU aid is not to be seen as a rival to Member States' bilateral aid programmes. Quite the contrary: EU institutions' aid is complementary to that of member states, and is designed as such.

4 An Overview of EU (LDC's) Development Policy
Friedrich Hamburger

The foundations for a fully fledged European development policy were laid at the creation of the European Economic Community in 1957. At that time Member States agreed to make a joint financial contribution to the economic and social development of their still-dependent territories, and allow them preferential access to the European market. This system was continued after their independence, in the form of a partnership agreement, and widened to include former territories of new Member States, and also other developing countries. This partnership, which came to be known by the African capital where the first Convention was signed, Lomé, has been adapted over the years to answer to new challenges. We are presently in the Fourth Lomé Convention, which was agreed in 1989 for a duration of ten years. Lomé's membership has steadily increased to encompass at present some 70 developing countries in Africa, the Caribbean and the Pacific (the ACP). In the near future we may even welcome the seventy-first member, South Africa, whose accession we are now negotiating, albeit on restricted terms.

In addition to the ACP, the European Union has more recently developed its relations with developing countries in other regions of the world, in particular in the Mediterranean, Latin America and with the countries in transition in Central and Eastern Europe and the former Soviet Union. Relations with the ACP countries remain, however, the cornerstone of the European development cooperation policy. The ACP countries receive about 60 per cent of annual disbursements made by the European Community to development cooperation.

Taken together, the European Community now provides roughly 4 billion ECU (or 5 billion dollars) a year for the benefit of some 100 developing countries across the globe. According to figures of the Development Assistance Committee (DAC) of the OECD, the European Community is thereby the only so-called 'multilateral donor' that has increased its share of development assistance, from some 19 per cent in 1981 to 25 per cent of total multilateral assistance in 1994. The full commitment of the European Union to the developing world is, however, even more tangibly expressed in terms of percentage of donors' GNP.

According to the same statistics, the European Union contributes 58 per cent of total Official Development Assistance by OECD DAC Members, even though it represents only 37 per cent of their total GNP.

The Maastricht Treaty defined the objectives of our development cooperation: sustainable development, poverty alleviation and the smooth and gradual integration of developing countries into the world economy. Where does Europe go from here?

In particular, since the agreement of our main development mechanism, the Fourth Lomé Convention, back in 1989, a number of unprecedented changes have taken place in the world. I do not think it is necessary to mention them in detail, but the political and economic liberalisation following the end of the Cold War and the conclusion of the Uruguay Round are certainly among the most important. Our development strategies need to be adapted to these changes, and respond to them. As a matter of fact, we used the mid-term review of Lomé IV to adapt our partnership to some of these new realities.

Let me consider a few issues, which I believe are key elements for our future development cooperation. In general terms, I believe that the challenges ahead of us require, more than in the past, a coherent donor approach. Therefore, donors should work together and ensure a true complementarity of their activities. Although I am thinking in this context first and foremost of those donors whom it is within Europe's power to influence, that is, the European Community and Member States, I believe that it is necessary to have a coherent approach between all donors, national, regional and multilateral.

Also our relationships with developing countries should become, more and more, partnerships of equals with mutual responsibilities. In this respect I think that Europe has a substantial experience to offer, our Lomé Conventions having been the first true partnership arrangements with developing countries in the world.

In the same context, conditionality in economic reform programmes should be reformulated better to foster recipient country commitment which we call 'ownership', increase the predictability of flows of conditional finance, and help reconcile short- and long-term requirements. This point is particularly important in the case of the least developed countries.

In general, and where possible, developing countries should themselves be in charge. This will require for certain countries an initial focus on capacity building. Also, good governance should become a serious focus of attention to ensure that the means at our partners' disposal are not used wrongly.

With the developing world becoming increasingly diverse, our responses may need to differ as well. Some countries are taking off by showing that more sustained economic growth is able to attract private investments, others are stagnating or even falling back into crisis as a result of internal or other conflicts.

The needs and the opportunities for these groups of countries are naturally not the same. Our support should be as much as possible tailor-made to the needs and potentialities of the individual countries. I believe in general terms our financial assistance should be geared more and more to the poorest. This means to the poorest countries and to the poorest parts of population within each country.

As regards our trade instruments, we will have to consider carefully whether we should not progress towards two-way free-trade arrangements with those countries which can support and benefit from them. We are proposing exactly such a relationship now with South Africa. Generous conditions of market access are not enough. We will need to assist partner countries to make themselves more competitive and increase their export earnings in various ways. These include a more favourable climate for private investment, strengthening investor confidence in the policy framework, more effective trade promotion, and private sector development.

Commissioner Prof. Pinheiro presented a Green Paper on our future relations with the ACP countries beyond the year 2000 in November 1996. The Green Paper is intended to launch a broad and open discussion with our partners, with the general public and all those institutions – non-governmental, academic and all sectors of civil society – interested in development cooperation. It will present a picture of our current relations, and options on where we might go from here. The Green Paper will address a number of key questions: strategy; the scope of future relations; the use of traditional instruments; aid and trade. It intends to build on what has been achieved so far, and adapt our policies where necessary.

Regarding strategy, the first issue to consider will be the role of Europe in North–South relations. In a changing international environment, where the US does not exercise leadership any more in North–South relations, and where Europe provides more than 50 per cent of global Official Development Assistance, the question is whether Europe should not assert greater leadership. The future relations with the ACP countries have to be considered particularly in this context. Presently, Europe is not only the largest donor to the ACP countries, but also for many of them their most important trading partner. And Europe appears still to be the preferred trading partner of Africa.

Another question of strategy concerns the geographical scope of EC–ACP relations. Given the continuing differentiation between the ACP countries, the question is whether there should be one successor of Lomé, or several. In other words, whether relations should be maintained within a single framework, such as Lomé, or whether other arrangements based on geographical location or level of development would be more effective.

As regards the scope of future relations, several issues need to be considered. They include questions relating to the areas of intervention: should competitiveness, investment, capacity building, private sector development, conflict prevention and conflict resolution receive more prominence than in the past?

Also on aid and trade policy a number of choices will need to be made. Aid has until now mainly been based on 'need'. Naturally, also in the future, the level of development should continue to be an important determinant for the amount of aid each ACP country will receive. As a matter of fact, I strongly believe that our aid should be focused on those that need it most. This means priority for the poorest countries and priority for the poorest parts of the population. However, given the increasing importance attached to issues such as democracy, good governance and structural adjustment, the question is whether in future additional allocation criteria should apply. In short, should aid be based on 'need' and on 'merit', as the disbursement of the eighth EDF in two tranches already suggests.

Still on aid, we presently have a large number of instruments. Each of these instruments has its own specific objectives, conditions, and procedures. In practice it is proving more and more difficult to handle these instruments in a coherent fashion in support of the individual development strategies of the ACP countries. Also, the different needs and opportunities of the ACP countries require increasing flexibility to tailor the EC's support to the specific requirements of individual countries. The question is, therefore, whether the EC should rationalise its instruments and provide at the same time a more flexible mechanism in support of the individual development strategies of ACP countries.

Finally, let me just say a few words on trade. In the world of the twenty-first century this part of our relations will become increasingly important. The main challenge in this area will be to find the proper response to the process of globalisation which is set to continue with technological advance and international liberalisation under the WTO. The options in this area range between the maintenance of the status quo to the introduction of progressive free-trade arrangements. That trade will prove to be a difficult issue is shown by the present trade negotiations with South Africa. For the ACP countries, South Africa holds a kind of pioneer position in this area, and its experiences can be useful to some of them.

What I have just mentioned are a number of fundamental issues which I believe would have to be thoroughly discussed before we prepare for the next round of negotiations. Whatever the outcome of these discussions, there are a number of unchallengeable principles on which, I believe, our relationship should continue to be based. These are: partnership between the EC and the ACP countries; ownership by the ACP countries of their development policies; security in terms of EC support to the ACP countries; and the predictability of external relations and aid flows.

In spite of the notion of aid fatigue which seems to dominate most of the public discussions on development nowadays, I would like to suggest more optimism for the end of this millennium. The new opportunities provided by the end of the ideological divide which marked this century and by the reform processes under way everywhere, as well as the globalisation of all spheres of human interest, should give us a new sense of purpose and commitment.

5 Europe's New Development Policy

Marjorie Lister

The relationship between the European Union and the developing countries (LDCs) has been called 'one of the most dynamic fields' in the whole range of EU politics.[1] This dynamism comes from the vast array of initiatives, contracts, and policies created by the European Community (now Union) since 1957. These range from the short-lived Arusha Convention in the 1960s, to the grandly named Global Mediterranean Policy of the 1970s and the long-time flagship of European development policy, the Lomé Convention. The latter, with 71 developing country members in Africa, the Caribbean and Pacific, was often described by the EU as a 'model' of development cooperation. However, pride of place in the EU's development policy has been taken since 1995 by the Barcelona Process, the fledgeling programme to establish a Euro-Mediterranean partnership and free-trade area between the EU and the countries of the southern Mediterranean basin. The Lomé Convention, by contrast, is now languishing under a cloud of uncertainty.

The shifting priorities of the European Union's development policy in the mid-1990s are summarised below:[2]

1. declining interest in the 71 African, Caribbean and Pacific (ACP) States;
2. declining interest in the poor countries of Central America;
3. a continuing gap between expressions of interest in Asia and activities in that region;
4. increasing interest in the neighbouring countries of the Mediterranean region; and
5. increasing interest in the growth areas of South America, notably the Southern Cone Common Market (Mercosur).

Since 80 per cent of the world's population live in developing countries, and as a group these countries' economies are growing faster than Europe's, the economic importance of developing countries is clear. However, for some developing countries, especially the least developed and

17

those in sub-Saharan Africa, the future is less hopeful. The apparent economic failure of sub-Saharan African countries in particular led to a climate of doubt and 'afropessimism' in the 1990s regarding their development prospects and the prospects for the Lomé Convention.

Although European development policy, taken as a whole, can be said to be dynamic, with changing policies and changing priorities and mechanisms, development has never been one of the EU's top priorities. The European Community (since 1993 Union) often reacted to events rather than following a coherent plan. The EU Member States have different concepts of development, different levels of commitment to it, and different ideas about how far the development process should be carried out through the EU.

In 1995 UN Secretary-General Boutros Boutros-Ghali called development 'the most important task facing humanity today' and asked for a new development agenda to make the next century 'the development century'.[3] But this view is not widely shared. Development is perceived in many quarters as a 'sunset industry'. The failure of the industrialised states to reach the UN's target of 0.7 per cent of GNP for aid has almost become an international norm. Development aid budgets are easy to cut. The viability of UNCTAD, UNIDO and UNESCO, and the financial soundness of the UN itself, are all in question.

European public opinion remains broadly supportive of development goals. A 1991 survey commissioned by the EU found that 82 per cent of Europeans were in favour of development cooperation, with just 12 per cent opposed.[4] Nevertheless, many development issues make headlines as obscure or uninteresting to the general public as 'Small Earthquake in Chile: Not Many Hurt'.[5] Few European citizens recognise the Lomé Convention by name or could differentiate its European Development Fund from internal EU regional development funds. Thus, the favourable climate of European public opinion is not transmitted into pressure for specific development programmes.

The major current theme of development theory is that it has reached an impasse,[6] stalemate, crisis or just a dead end. It has even been argued that contemporary development studies became so inward-looking or self-obsessed that 'the theory replaced the thing as the primary focus of enquiry'.[7] Development studies is not the only field of social science where the study of the field may have replaced the study of the object, but this problem suggests a general lack of success in achieving development goals.

In practical terms the failure of aid and development policies in sub-Saharan Africa in particular is widely accepted. UNCTAD calculated that it would take more than a decade at growth rates of 3 per cent or more for much of Africa to achieve the levels of real per capita income of 20 years ago.[8] As one of the major donors to Africa, the European Union shares in this disappointing outcome. When compared with the $142 billion dollars (at 1992 prices) of aid which entered sub-Saharan Africa during the decade 1980–90, the average decline in GDP of 1 per cent per capita in the region looks a very poor return.[9] Linking the intellectual problem of development theory with the observable problems of Africa, Colin Leys observed: 'both development theory and Africa are in deep trouble'.[10]

Despite four decades of development aid and almost two decades of structural adjustment, the indicators for Africa are disappointing. Africa's share of world trade declined by more than half from 1980 to 1995, from 5 per cent to a mere 2.2 per cent.[11] None of the supposed development panaceas of the 1980s and 90s, including structural adjustment, the operation of the free market, or directing aid through non-governmental organisations[12] has proved altogether satisfactory, although all of them can contribute to improving the development process. Even the most apparently laudable intentions of state-led development plans, such as population control, may have the unwanted side-effects of disempowering the women they should help.[13]

Economists too have contributed to the 'impasse' debate. Stanford Professor Paul Krugman took an extreme view. Not only was there an impasse, development theory had absolutely nothing to offer: 'There is no wisdom on economic development, and there are no wise men'.[14] Even the outstanding examples of development in the latter half of this century, the East Asian tigers, to Krugman offered no model for contemporary developing countries: 'the policies followed in rapidly growing Asian economies have been sufficiently varied and ambiguous that observers who are determined to draw conclusions can find whatever they want...There are no obvious lessons about what governments in less successful regions should do.'[15]

Nevertheless, a more thorough examination reveals that the variety of policies followed in East Asia did share common elements: 'There is now general agreement that the governments of these countries intervened heavily in all spheres of the economy in order to achieve rapid economic growth and fast industrialization.'[16] Thus although the Asian tigers may provide no single, easily replicable recipe for other developing areas, they do give a series of lessons about government assistance to markets in different environments and with different objectives, ranging from security to export growth.

Although the East Asian economies in the past 20 years boomed up to 1997 in a fairly liberal and open world market, other developing countries may not be able to benefit from any amount of market liberalisation. This is analogous to some firms which cannot compete successfully in global markets and go bankrupt. Likewise some countries are unable to produce any globally competitive products. Colin Leys over-estimated the extent to which this idea is generally accepted, but the point that some states – the small, poor, island, landlocked, disadvantaged, ethnically divided – cannot contend in the increasingly sophisticated international market seems justified in practice:[17]

Most observers accept that significant parts of the former Third World, including most of sub-Saharan Africa, are more likely to regress than to advance in the new global economy; it is in the nature of an unregulated competitive system that this will happen. Not every country has the capacity to compete in the market; a few will succeed, while others will decline and some will collapse into civil war or anarchy, as Uganda, Angola, Mozambique, Liberia and Rwanda already have in Africa, at different times.

Among the most striking examples of countries which face difficulties in competing successfully on the world market are some of the EU's sugar-producing partners. Since 1975 ACP countries have been given quotas at above world-market prices for sugar they exported to Europe. At the same time, a conflicting policy of high European sugar production and subsidised sugar exports tended to undermine world prices.

Under the liberalising influence of the GATT, the EU agreed to reduce its subsidised sugar exports by 40 000 tonnes, but this is probably insufficient to benefit other sugar producers very much.[18] MacDonald estimated that through the change from a variable import levy to a tariff system, ACP sugar producers as a group would lose over $123 million US dollars in income transfers in the year 2000.[19] The countries which would suffer most from this EU policy reform were those most dependent on sugar for their foreign exchange earnings, that is, the small island economies. These countries will also find it hardest to diversify into other kinds of production.[20] The Lomé objective of reducing price and earnings volatility is also likely to suffer, to the disadvantage of EU as well as ACP states.

THE EU's DEVELOPMENT ENVIRONMENT

One feature that makes European development policy important is the size of its aid programme. From just 7 per cent in 1970, by 1994 over 17 per cent of the member states' aid was directed through the European Union. While national aid budgets shrink, the EU's share of its members' aid policies continues growing. After the World Bank, the EU is the second largest multilateral aid donor.[21]

The European Union is trying to re-evaluate and reformulate a development relationship with the African, Caribbean and Pacific States and its southern Mediterranean neighbours during a time of unparalleled uncertainty. On the one hand, it is clear that the international environment of the late 1990s is vastly different from that of the 1970s when the first Lomé Convention, with 46 developing countries, was first signed. The possibilities of the 1970s, notably the prospect of a New International Economic Order designed to redistribute wealth in favour of developing countries and commodity producers, are no longer discussed. Even the idea of using a peace dividend – the funds made available in the West as the end of the Cold War made lower military spending possible – for development purposes has evaporated. Instead governments have cut taxes to please voters or found new expenses such as cleaning up the environment around military bases and buying more expensive and sophisticated weapons. In their efforts to save money and reduce deficits, governments have cut budgets (including aid budgets) instead of increasing them.

No longer is decolonisation, the overriding issue of the 1950s when the Part IV Association of the Treaty of Rome was formulated, of fundamental concern. The few remaining, scattered colonies of the developed countries show little sign of seeking independence – whose results in many cases have proved disappointing. George Drower argued that Britain's dependent territories should now be considered as a 'permanent empire'.[22]

Faced with a variety of crises in Africa, the incumbent British Foreign Secretary Douglas Hurd called in 1992 for the UN to take on an 'imperial role' in distressed countries such as Somalia.[23] Understandably, this produced an unhappy reaction in many developing countries, and the idea was not repeated in Mr Hurd's address to the UN's General Assembly a few days later, nor did it form any part of the New World Order programme.[24]

Despite the largely hostile reaction to Mr Hurd's proposal, the 'imperial idea' has not been completely abandoned. At least one European thinker argued that not only should the remaining dependent territories not be de-colonized, the old European empires should be reinstituted. In order to prevent emigration of unacceptable migrants and to establish better government in the ex-colonies, former Oxford professor Norman Stone called for the 'enlightened re-imperialism' of Africa by Europe. Such views may be partly tongue-in-cheek; Stone's own admission that European empires made mistakes the first time round hardly recommends trying the same strategy again.[25] Nevertheless, the popular expression of the idea of re-imperialization shows widespread disappointment with contemporary political and economic problems in Africa and with the failure of the international community to resolve them.

The UK Overseas Development Administration's introductory information sheet rightly recognizes the origins of aid policy in colonial policy: 'The British Government's responsibility for the development of its colonies on a continuing basis was first recognised in 1929 by the Colonial Development Act.'[26] In the 1980s it became fashionable to eschew moral arguments for aid and arguments for aid based on post-colonial responsibility.[27] However, as noted above, European public opinion has remained in favour of aid, both in terms of private giving and official development assistance.[28] Recently, in a powerful study of international aid, David Lumsdaine argued that 'Many converging lines of evidence show that economic foreign aid cannot be explained on the basis of donor states' political and economic interests, and that humanitarian concern in the donor countries formed the main basis of support for aid.'[29] Although altruism in aid is normally mixed with other motives – political, economic, strategic – the moral underpinnings of development cooperation cannot be discounted.

Europe's goodwill towards the developing regions remains real, but the best way to organize and manage its relationships with developing areas is in doubt. The way European commercial, political and development objectives should be balanced is also at issue. The European Commission's Report for the Reflection Group on preparing the ground for the Intergovernmental Conference of 1996 made clear the EU's two top priorities: reforming internal decision-making and taking in the neighbouring countries of central and eastern Europe.[30] Development cooperation received limited attention. The primary emphasis in the report was placed on attaining greater coordination between the development policies of the member states and the EU in order to achieve 'economies of scale'. The Commission envisaged 'the establishment of medium-term strategies for each country and involving the concentration of resources on agreed priority objectives'.[31] In addition to expanding the Commission's central coordinating role, the report argued in favour of the reduction from unanimity to a qualified majority for adopting multi-annual comprehensive programmes (for example, for the Mediterranean region) which set out the means and objectives of development cooperation for both the Community and the Member States.

This report raises a number of questions. Is the EU's objective of combining its development policies primarily about development effectiveness or more about prestige – about making its development policy 'more visible, more credible and more influential – particularly in comparison with other donors'?[32] While making EU aid as cohesive as US, Japanese or World Bank aid might enhance the EU's foreign policy image, its value in development terms is more ambiguous. It might lead to the funding of unsuitable but visible prestige projects like the Pergau Dam. An excessive desire to be more influential than other donors could lead to sacrificing development goals for political favours.

COORDINATION AND COHERENCE

The questions regarding greater coordination of EU Member States' development aid programmes include

1. Would coordination/amalgamation be an excuse for cost-cutting?
2. Is the European Commission – which is not widely known for its efficiency or transparency[33] – administratively able to coordinate the development policies of 15 Member States successfully? It has been persuasively argued that 'institutional capacities at the Commission already do not keep pace with the explosion in the tasks to be performed'.[34]
3. Is a multiplicity of development funders desirable – given that no one development programme has a monopoly of expertise?

In summary, the worst-case result of greater coordination of development policies would be one unified European development programme, not well funded, not well administered and seeking only a lowest-common-denominator of development activities. The best-case scenario – wherein EU member countries would maintain or increase the total volume of their development aid while being effectively coordinated by the European Commission into a progressive development policy – seems less plausible. Certainly greater communication and experience sharing between EU member governments' aid programmes would be desirable, whether or not this eventually leads to more central coordination or administration from the EU institutions.

The objective set out in the Treaty of Maastricht of making development policy coherent with other EU policies appears quite ambitious. No longer should the EU export or 'dump' beef on West Africa while trying to aid the livestock industry there; no longer should the EU produce excess sugar for export while trying to raise the living standards of ACP sugar producers. The objective of increasing ACP industrial development would not be vititated by EU commercial concerns. In the case of beef exports to West Africa, the European Commission clearly recognized the problem: 'European exports seriously hurt local production, the regional trade and livestock development projects financed by the EDF.'[35] A solution was less easy to devise: from 1993 some reduction of export subsidies for beef was agreed, but this only ameliorated the problem. An NGO and European Parliament proposal to address these issues more fully through a consultation mechanism within the European Commission was not accepted.

Although greater policy coherence could clearly produce benefits in the example of beef above, a worst case interpretation could be put on the objective of policy coherence. The Catholic Institute for International Relations argued: 'is not a commitment to coherence merely a pledge to subordinate development policy to other major European objectives so that the developmental will necessarily lose out in any serious clash of interests?'[36] Development policy might consistently lose out when agricultural or industrial interests conflicted with development objectives. When in 1996 the EU refused aid to a South African steel plant, it seemed that CIIR could be right: industrial interests took precedence over developmental ones.[37]

Christiane Loquai rightly noted that the concern to develop greater coordination between the aid programmes of the member states and greater coherence between development and other EU policies dates back to the 1970s. The debate on this subject may be more comprehensive and systematic than previously as the EU tries to improve coordination in international fora, in policy-making and in implementation.[38] But the EU still lacks even a common definition of policy coherence.[39]

The pilot project established in 1994 to improve coordination between EU donors in Bangladesh, Costa Rica, Côte d'Ivoire, Ethiopia, Mozambique and Peru has not yet reported; neither have coordination experiments in sectors such as AIDS and HIV, education and training, or food security been completed. Further coordination may remain difficult as member states want to maintain their individual prerogatives and lack a clear idea of how much coordination and coherence they want.

REGIONALISM, GLOBALISM AND DEVELOPMENT

One of the major questions to be answered regarding EU aid policy is its regional focus. The reasons for this are historical: Latin America gained its independence a century earlier than Africa, and its main former colonial powers – Spain and Portugal – were not part of the original European Community. The first focus of EU development policy was on sub-Saharan Africa which, with its great natural resources, looked in the 1950s like the best international bet for economic development as well as being a politically dynamic region.

For a variety of political, historical and geo-strategic reasons the European Community built up strong links with the countries of Africa, the Caribbean and Pacific. However, as the development prospects of these countries deteriorated (especially for Africa) while the EC's aspirations to a global role increased, questions have arisen over the reasonableness of the EU's system of regional development cooperation, notably in the four successive Lomé Conventions. But what would the abandonment of the Lomé policy be likely to mean? Several probable results would follow.

The down-grading of sub-Saharan Africa

The poor countries of Africa, which have large debts and few immediate development prospects, would fall to the bottom of the EU's development agenda. Their position of relative privilege in the EU's development policy would disappear as other, more economically promising, regions received greater attention.

The loss of political cooperation

Lomé may never have been exactly a 'model of cooperation' between North and South, but it was a form of ongoing political dialogue. The loss or reduction of such a dialogue – carried out in the various institutions of Lomé such as the Joint Consultative Assembly, the Committee of Ambassadors, the Joint Council of Ministers, and the Centre for Industrial Development – is ultimately undesirable. Lomé is the most successful long-term example of a region-to-region dialogue Europe has produced.

Compared to the Euro–Arab dialogue, or dialogues with ASEAN, Latin America or Central America, Lomé was deeper and more durable.

The loss of the regional development model

Development initiatives aimed at a global scale have been useful but not unambiguously effective. The present international argument has been called liberalisation or globalisation versus development.[40] That is, globalisers argue that since development policies have not so far eradicated poverty, such policies should be abandoned in favour of the free market. Only global capitalism, they maintain, the opening and liberalisation of markets, will accomplish development. However, as discussed on page 20, this view is not fully justified. Many poor countries do not prosper in the competitive, global market.

The alternative to globalisation and liberalisation for developing countries is not global development policies alone. Global-level initiatives ranging from the Brandt Report to the Common Fund for Commodities and the Generalised System of Preferences have had limited success in achieving development, leaving plenty of scope for supplementary regional initiatives – like Lomé. The global approach could be considered as an outgrowth of modernist development theory – a meta-theory which sought to be applicable to all countries in all conditions at all times. By contrast, Lomé might not be anachronistic[41] but instead a forward-looking system, allowing for a considerable diversity of approaches within it.

Fawcett and Hurrell argued that increasing regionalism is a central fact of post-Cold War politics. Without mentioning the Lomé Convention, they contended that 'A central characteristic of many of the most important examples of the new regionalism is that they span the divide between developed and developing countries.'[42] Thus, with its developed–developing country structure, Lomé is comparable to the new regional organisations such as the North Atlantic Free Trade Area (NAFTA) and the Asia-Pacific Economic Cooperation organisation (APEC), which have been setting international trends in the 1990s. So pervasive is the trend towards establishing or strengthening regional organizations that it could be argued that if the Lomé group of European, African, Caribbean and Pacific states did not now exist, it would almost have to be created.[43]

A growing sense of regional identity can be found in many areas of the world, not least Europe. This new regionalism can co-exist happily with globalism. Regionalism can be the supplement or partner of globalism and not its alternative. Regional organisations can be the handmaidens of the UN, not competitors. Global goals regarding the environment, security or development may be best achieved through regional organisations. A global order can be based on the relatively more integrated building blocks of regional organisations. As Hurrell observed, 'The old controversy over the relative merits of regionalism and globalism has become increasingly obsolete.'[44] The question is not one of regionalism versus globalism, but how best to combine the two processes.[45]

The idea that a development policy must be global to be ethical, rational or effective may die hard. The Catholic Institute for International Relations, for instance, took the European Union to task over this issue: 'European development policy is fragmented; it is regional rather than global in vision; different principal criteria and strategic goals affect policy towards different regions...this fragmented approach cannot adequately deal with the global challenges of poverty and the environment.'[46] Whatever the intellectual appeal of globalism, there is no sign that a global approach alone is adequately dealing with the challenges of poverty, the status of women or the environment. Participating in regional or pan-regional organizations such as the Lomé Convention does not preclude the EU Member States from participating fully in the UN's Environment Programme (UNEP), UNICEF or other global organisations.

Some critics of Lomé policy have not argued in favour of globalising Lomé, but merely of changing the recipients. Lingnau reckoned that South Africa should not be included in Lomé as this would 'strain cooperation', that is, South Africa could export industrial goods to Europe.[47] But the EU itself has taken a more positive view than this, negotiating a twin-track arrangement whereby South Africa gains admission to Lomé, but without the trade preferences or Stabex. Excluding South Africa (of great disadvantage to its SACU and SADC partners who are Lomé members) would make nonsense of the whole thrust of Lomé regional policy to incorporate black Africa.[48] Recently, it appears that the EU's efforts to create a free-trade area with South Africa have faltered.[49] But it may be that some modifications of the EU stance will ultimately be acceptable to South Africa.

Lingnau advocated the proposal for including all least developed countries under Lomé – for example, Bangladesh, Afghanistan – which would greatly alter the Lomé centre of gravity and change the nature of the dialogue. Instead, a policy of 'open regionalism' with regard to development would mean Europe could also give these countries the equivalent development assistance they require, but not necessarily within the Lomé framework. The proposal to create a Lomé Convention for least developed countries alone[50] would lose the benefits outlined above. With fewer of the developing countries which have good economic or political prospects, such a regime of the poorest might have a very low priority indeed. The main disappointment of the Lomé regime has been its failure to lift the ACP countries as a group into higher levels of development and standards of living, but improving the standards of the least developing countries might prove equally or even more frustrating.

The loss of a variety of development instruments

In fact, Lomé's development instruments are so diverse and complex that they could use some pruning.[51] The Sugar Protocol, project aid and aid for structural adjustment, for instance, each embody quite different development philosophies (or eras). But all of these could – with improvements – remain useful. The operational problems and anomalies of the Stabex and Sysmin systems, however, are sufficient to call them into question. As remnants of the New International Economic Order programme of the 1970s, their failure to function efficiently or to do the job of commodity price or export earnings stabilisation suggests that these funds might be used more effectively elsewhere.[52] Aid to commodity production and diversification, and aid to mineral production could be subsumed under project aid, eliminating them as a separate and often awkward area of administration. By working in a great many areas from health to education, transport infrastructure to agricultural development and energy, the EU can miss out on creating enough 'critical mass' in one area to produce ongoing or sustainable development in the recipient country.[53] Furthermore, one of the main points running through a review of EU aid was that European Commission staff were not expert in many issue-areas of development including gender, poverty reduction, environment and population.[54] Concentrating on fewer sectors or mechanisms for development cooperation would help the EU to build up a critical mass of projects or support in those areas and to develop relevant staff expertise.

The loss of Lomé as a political animal

When Lomé is described as an aid and trade pact or a system of development cooperation, its political and institutional aspects are often overlooked. It would be surprising if the past four decades of cooperation between Europe and its partner developing countries had not created a unique political identity. In political science terminology, this is called an international regime. The study of international regimes examines forms of cooperation in the international system.

Regimes are 'sets of rules that define social practices, assign roles to the participants in these practices, and govern relations among the occupants of those roles'.[55] Regimes can be as broad and inclusive as the United Nations or functionally specific like agreements on whaling or the depletion of the ozone layer. Regimes operate as nodes of organisation within the technically anarchic international system, giving it important elements of orderliness. *Inter alia* regimes create stability, increase the flow of information among the partners and may reduce the intensity of their conflicts.[56] Or they may provide no more than an orderly approach to a given set of problems. Forming effective international regimes can be difficult and may commonly take ten years or more.[57]

It is true that the study of international regimes comprises more a perspective or 'a research programme' than a firm body of knowledge.[58] Arguably, more has been said and written about the aspects and processes of international regimes which are not well understood than about those which are. Despite these caveats, analysing the EU–ACP relationship in terms of regime theory does yield useful insights.

In terms of the EU–ACP relationship, a fundamental regime reorganisation, such as globalisation for instance, might mean the regime would no longer function effectively. It has been argued that for the European Union itself the most important source of integration and stability is the habit of cooperation among its member states. For the EU–ACP relationship, this is also the case. Any fundamental changes in the Lomé system could risk doing away with this valuable habit of cooperation.

International regimes such as the Lomé Convention can be described as embedded or nested within a broad network of norms and institutions. The more general or higher-order norms operate as frames of reference for the more specific regimes. Regimes refer to these higher norms for their strength and stability.[59] In the case of the Lomé Convention, it can be seen as embedded within the wider international regime of development cooperation. Lomé is a part of the general international effort for development whose norms inform *inter alia* the UN, the OECD, the World Bank and the US Agency for International Development (US-AID). In the 1970s the Lomé system was at least partly nested in the ultimately unsuccessful efforts by developing countries to achieve a New International Economic Order and global 'third world' solidarity. More recently, the end of the Cold War has brought to the fore the international norms of human rights and 'good' or democratic governance. The Lomé system, again, has positioned itself within this broader regime, adopting the prevalent international norms and standards of human rights. As long as Lomé can incorporate new international norms or embed itself in global regimes in this way, its durability should be enhanced. The next section analyses how the Lomé regime has moved towards intensifying political conditionality on issues of human rights and the good governance agenda.

DEMOCRACY, HUMAN RIGHTS AND THE PROBLEM OF CONDITIONALITY

In the 1980s and 1990s donors increasingly attached economic and latterly political conditions to their aid programmes. In the Lomé system conditions have always existed: the first one is to join the Convention. In the cases of Mozambique and Angola, for instance, the European Commission exerted considerable effort to get these countries to fulfil this minimum condition and sign the Lomé contract. In practice, a minimum respect for human rights was also a condition for receiving aid, and human rights violators like Idi Amin faced aid cut-backs.[60] Stephan Haggard's observation about Lomé that 'little is demanded of the partners who are developing countries' has certainly not been true in the 1990s.[61]

The 1995 mid-term review of Lomé IV made political conditionality still more strict and more transparent. But even in earlier periods the ACP had to participate in a political-bureaucratic dialogue with the European Commission and to devote considerable administrative effort to project identification and management (regardless of whether the projects were ultimately very successful.) Article 5 of the Lomé IV Convention as revised by the agreement signed in Mauritius on 4 November 1995 made 'respect for human rights, democratic principles and the rule of law' into an 'essential element' or legally enforceable condition for receiving aid.

This increased aid conditionality has been criticised by many development specialists. Glenn Brigaldino argued that aid effectiveness depended on the 'dropping of non-developmental, political and economic aid objectives of donors'.[62] However, the possibility of the EU reducing its aid conditionality is very unlikely. As donors seek to get better value for money for their aid, to see development indicators improve and projects succeed, 'the current trend is toward increasing conditionality with an ever-higher degree of political interference'.[63] In view of the virtual international consensus in favour of aid conditionality, the EU might be better advised to develop workable forms of conditionality with its developing country partners rather than to abandon explicit conditionality altogether. As noted above, adopting the prevailing norms of the international system is one factor which may help the Lomé regime to survive.

In practice, aid conditionality is normally exercised with some flexibility both by the EU and other donors. The European Commission pointed out in reply to the European Court of Auditors that, regarding the conditions contained in the economic policy framework for the partner developing countries:

> Experience shows that these measures have never been fully complied with, and the Commission, if it adhered strictly to compliance with each of those measures, could in every case refuse disbursement ... assessment is based as much on a government's efforts to implement the programmed measures as on actual implementation within the timetable stipulated. Since, in the majority of programmes, priority budgetary support goes to the social sectors, a total freezing of support in the event of non-compliance with conditions would impose a very heavy burden.[64]

Since 1991 the EU has given increasing importance to issues of human rights, democracy and the rule of law. The EU's explicit policy is to focus on incentive and positive measures rather than negative measures (sanctions). Nevertheless, the EU suspended cooperation with a significant number of ACP countries over human rights problems in the 1990s. The OECD cited Equatorial Guinea, Haiti, Liberia, Malawi, Somalia, Sudan, Togo and Zaire as experiencing suspensions.[65] Niger and Nigeria joined this list in 1996, so that in the 1990s over 14 per cent of the 71 ACP countries were subject to negative measures.

The positive measures for democracy, human rights and good governance funded by the EU include 143 human rights projects in developing countries, 39 per cent of which were in the ACP. These involved strengthening the rule of law, supporting the electoral process, supporting local information media, helping vulnerable groups such as ethnic minorities, and giving training and information about human rights. The quality and success of these projects is not yet known. At present six Commission staff are responsible for the EU's human rights and democracy projects.[66]

It has been argued that the EU should not now cooperate at all with developing countries with poor human rights records or 'criminal' regimes.[67] Although initially attractive, the practice of stopping aid to badly governed countries could harm the most vulnerable people in those countries. Instead of this drastic measure, aid should be directed to benefit the poorest sections of the population. This would both fulfil the Lomé objective of decentralised cooperation (Article 12a of the agreement above) and fulfil the Maastricht Treaty's objective of alleviating poverty in developing countries.

One recent set of proposals for the reform of aid conditionality bore several elements of resemblance to the existing operation of the Lomé Convention, but without specifically mentioning Lomé.[68] Han Singer's suggested reforms of World Bank, IMF and other donors' conditionalities included greater flexibility in conditions, and composing conditions in terms of general objectives rather than specific instruments. The Commission's statement quoted above reveals its acknowledged operational flexibility, a flexibility sometimes greater than the European Court of Auditors would accept. The text of the Lomé Convention disposes of many more objectives than specific instruments of economic or political conditionality. The Lomé system has no trouble coming up with idealistic goals and objectives; the challenge is to prioritise and implement them, giving the Lomé partnership a better development outcome.

Another of Professor Singer's proposals – for making conditionality a two-way process – sounds very much like the Lomé formula: 'There should be more of a development contract between donors and recipients rather than unilateral conditionality'.[69] Since 1963, European development aid to Africa has been based on an explicit contract. The contractual basis of the now much-expanded Lomé Convention still exists, although it is currently widely believed that power within the Lomé contract has swung further towards Europe and away from the African, Caribbean and Pacific signatories. That is, the process is not fully 'two-way' but is more than one-way.

Another proposal from Hans Singer reflects one of the main concerns of the OECD. Singer argued that an independent investigation of the development programme should be available. The OECD report emphasized the need for more consistent evaluations of the whole range of European Union aid programmes and the continuing need to incorporate their findings into 'best practice'.[70] The European Court of Auditors does annually investigate and report on the European development programme, but more detailed work from independent evaluators could be beneficial, along with greater public availability of the results.

The proposal that conditionality 'should be pragmatically adjusted to the specific circumstances of each country and each situation' accords with standard EU practice. The European Commission attempts to reflect current conditions on the ground in its aid programming, creating a National Indicative Plan for each country. Like other donors, the EU must strike a balance between imposing too much political and economic conditionality and settling for too little.

The resemblance of the proposals above to the actual practice of EU–ACP cooperation suggests, again, that if some aspects at least of the Lomé Convention didn't exist, they would indeed have to be created.

CONCLUSION

In summary, despite its shortcomings European development cooperation still has many features to recommend it. Maintaining trade preferences for poor commodity-dependent economies is one challenge for Lomé. Streamlining, focusing and improving its aid disbursement is another. To these ends greater de-centralisation of decision-making and improvements in the staffing of the European Commission's development directorate should be undertaken.

Without an alternative plan that not only appears fairer or more rational on paper, but also can be seen to work successfully, abandoning the Lomé development regime is premature. As a recent evaluation of EU aid found, there were many failures of EU agricultural aid in Ethiopia, but the answer was not to give up: 'having put its hand to the plough, the EC/EU should build on its experience to find effective and sustainable solutions'.[71]

The Lomé Convention has taken on a difficult task: to improve the conditions of some of the world's poorest and most troubled countries. Lomé as a whole has had its failures, but nevertheless the EU should continue to 'keep its hand to the plough'. Although its development objectives have not yet been accomplished, the Lomé Convention so far offers the best framework through which this may be done successfully in the future.

The 1996 report on European Union aid by the Development Assistance Committee (DAC) of the OECD had three main themes. One theme was scathing criticisms of various inadequacies of the policy: wasted resources owing to the 'absence of a defined sustainable development strategy, administrative weaknesses, and inefficient recipient governments' (p. 23) or 'The overall policy with respect to gender is not easy to apprehend' (p. 44).[72] But alongside virtually every criticism of EU aid practice in the report is a reference to 'the significant progress that the European Commission has made in its development cooperation management since the last DAC Review in 1991'.[73] Perhaps more important than the specific criticisms or the references to considerable recent improvements, is the DAC's strong endorsement of the Lomé project as a whole:

> The Lomé Convention is an advanced example of co-operation between developed and developing countries in a long-term arrangement combining a range of instruments in aid, trade, co-operation in socio-economic sectors, and permanent dialogue on several levels.[74]

An alternative framework for European development policy – separating the regions of Africa, the Caribbean and Pacific or including only least developed countries in a post-Lomé agreement – would reduce the political importance of the new pact(s) to Europe. A radically new framework would abolish the positive habits of cooperation established under Lomé in favour of an untested new system, starting its new programme of cooperation from scratch. In the light of current conditions of uncertainty, and the lack of good alternatives provided by development theory, keeping the fundamental structure of the Lomé Convention intact seems the wisest available course. The European Development Commissioner Pinheiro was recently quoted as saying that the 'ACP states are clearly not much in fashion'.[75] Without the Lomé regime, these 'unfashionable' ACP states could well get a worse deal out of the EU than is presently *in situ*.

Renewing or re-inventing the Lomé Convention in the year 2000 might not make the next century 'the Development Century', but without a suitable successor to Lomé IV (bis), there is less chance that the popular predictions for a forthcoming 'Pacific Century', a further 'American Century' or a new 'European Century' will be joined by a 'Development Century'.

Notes

1. Loquai, Christiane, 'The Europeanisation of Development Cooperation: Coordination, Complementarity, Coherence', European Centre for Development Policy Management, Brussels, Working Paper No. 13, October 1996, p. 1.
2. Lister, M., 'Europe Looks South: European Development Policy at the End of the Millennium', *Internet Journal of African Studies*, April 1997, http://www.brad.ac.uk/research/ijas/ (forthcoming).
3. Boutros-Ghali, Boutros, *An Agenda for Development*, New York, United Nations, pp. 1–2.
4. 'The Lomé Convention in focus', *The Courier*, Brussels, No. 158, July–August 1996, p. 33.
5. Toye, John, *Dilemmas of Development*, 2nd ed., Oxford, Blackwell, 1993, p. 21. This was chosen by *Times* sub-editors as the least interesting headline.
6. Scott, Catherine, *Gender and Development*, Boulder, Lynne Rienner, 1995, p. 3.
7. *Ibid.*, p. 3, quoting Samuel Huntington.
8. 'Trade and Development Report 1996', *UNCTAD Bulletin*, No. 37, July–September 1996, p. 2.
9. Ryrie, William, 'Address by Sir William Ryrie', Development Studies Association Annual Conference, University of Reading, 18 September 1996.
10. Leys, Colin, *The Rise and Fall of Development Theory*, London, James Curry, 1996, p. 1.
11. Hawkins, Tony, 'Silver lining's dark image', *Financial Times*, 27 September 1996.
12. Edwards, Michael and Hulme, David, *Non-Governmental Organisations – Performance and Accountability*, London, Earthscan, 1996.
13. Correa, Sonia, *Population and Reproductive Rights*, London, Zed Books, 1994.
14. Krugman, Paul, 'Cycles of Conventional Wisdom on Economic Development', *International Affairs*, Vol. 71, No. 4, 1995, p. 732 (whether Krugman excluded the possibility of wise women is not altogether clear).
15. *Ibid.*, p. 731.
16. Singh, Ajit, 'How did East Asia Grow So Fast?', *UNCTAD Bulletin*, No. 32, May–June 1995, p. 8.
17. Leys, Colin, 'The Crisis in "Development Theory"', *New Political Economy*, Vol. 1, No. 1, March 1996, p. 42.
18. MacDonald, S., 'Reform of the EU's Sugar Policies and the ACP Countries', *Development Policy Review*, Vol. 14, No. 2, June 1996, p. 135.
19. *Ibid.*, p. 145.
20. *Ibid.*, p. 145.
21. OECD Development Assistance Committee, 'Development Cooperation Review Series: European Community', Summary of Development Cooperation Review Series, Paris, 1995.
22. Drower, G., *Britain's Dependent Territories*, Aldershot, Dartmouth, 1992.
23. Bevins, A., 'Hurd urges UN to take "imperial" role', *Independent*, 19 September 1992.

Europe's New Development Policy

24. Editorial, 'The cost of a mandate', *Independent*, 23 September 1992.
25. Stone, Norman, 'Why the Empire must strike back', *Observer*, 18 August 1996.
26. Overseas Development Administration, *Overseas Development*, London, August 1996.
27. Riddell, Roger, 'The Ethics of Foreign Aid', *Development Policy Review*, Vol. 4, No. 1, March 1986.
28. Lister, Marjorie, 'European Aid: a Response', *DSA Forum*, No. 41, September 1992.
29. Lumsdaine, David, *Moral Vision in International Politics*, Princeton, Princeton University Press, 1993, p. 3.
30. European Commission, *Commission Report for the Reflection Group*, Brussels, 1995.
31. *Ibid.*, pp. 56–7.
32. *Ibid.*, p. 56.
33. Stewart, Frances, 'Europe 1992 and Development Studies', *DSA Forum*, No. 40, May 1992.
34. Bossuyt, Jean (1994) 'Phased Programming of the Lomé Funds: Lessons from Current EU and ACP Experience', *Policy Management Brief*, Brussels, European Centre for Development Policy Management, No. 2, July 1994.
35. Development Assistance Committee of the OECD, 'European Community', Development Cooperation Review Series, No. 12, Paris, OECD, 1996, p. 39.
36. Catholic Institute for International Relations (CIIR), *Continental Shift: Europe's Policies Towards the South*, London, Comment Series, 1996, p. 11.
37. Wolf, Julie, 'No EU loan for South Africa Steel Plant', *Guardian*, 21 September 1996.
38. Development Assistance Committee of the OECD, 'European Community', 1996, p. 38; Loquai, 'Europeanisation of Development Cooperation', 1996, p. 38.
39. *Ibid.*, Loquai, p. 26.
40. Cumberbatch, Lingston, 'Are Globalisation and Development Mutually Exclusive?', *Beyond Lomé IV: Exploring Options for Future ACP–EU Cooperation*, Brussels, European Centre for Development Policy Management, Policy Management Report No. 6, October 1996, p. 68.
41. Frisch, Dieter, 'The Future of the Lomé Convention: Initial Reflections on Europe's Africa Policy after the Year 2000', European Centre for Development Policy Management, Working paper No. 11, Brussels, 1996, p. 2, considers Lomé not anachronistic on other grounds.
42. Fawcett, L., and Hurrell, A., 'Introduction', in Fawcett, L., and Hurrell, A. (eds), *Regionalism in World Politics*, Oxford, Oxford University Press, 1995, pp. 3–4.
43. Compare Cumberbatch, 'Are Globalisation and Development Mutually Exclusive?', p. 70.
44. Fawcett, L., 'Regionalism in Historical Perspective' in Fawcett and Hurrell, *Regionalism*, 1995, p. 19.
45. Fawcett, L., and Hurrell, A., 'Conclusion: Regionalism and International Order' in *ibid*.

46. CIIR, *Continental Shift*, 1996, p. 18.

47. Lingnau, Hildegard, 'Perspectives on Lomé Cooperation', Maastricht, European Centre for Development Policy Management Working Paper No. 12, May 1996, p. 9.

48. Lister, Marjorie, *The European Community and the Developing World*, Aldershot, Avebury, 1988 and 1990, Ch. 6.

49. Matthews, Roger and Southey, Caroline, 'South Africa to reject EU terms for trade deal', *Financial Times*, 15 January 1997, p. 4.

50. CIIR, *Continental Shift*, 1996.

51. As noted by Ambassador Lingston Cumberbatch of Trinidad and Tobago in 'Are Globalisation and Development Mutually Exclusive?', p. 70: 'There are too many provisions in Lomé IV which merely make good reading for the few people who bother to read them but have no practical effect as they are never implemented.'

52. Lister, Marjorie, *The European Union and the South*, London, Routledge, 1997, Ch.4.

53. Institute of Development Studies (IDS), University of Sussex and Institute of Development Research (IDR), Addis Ababa University, *An Evaluation of Development Cooperation between the European Union and Ethiopia, 1976–1994*, June 1996, p. 52.

54. Development Assistance Committee of the OECD, 'European Community', 1996.

55. Young, Oran, 'International Regime Initiation', *International Studies Notes*, Vol. 19, No. 3, Fall 1994, pp. 43–4.

56. Rittberger, Volker, *International Regimes in East–West Politics*, London, Pinter, 1990, p. 5.

57. Young, 'International Regime Initiation', p. 44.

58. 'Editor's Introduction', Rittberger, V., with P. Mayer (eds), *Regime Theory and International Relations*, Oxford, Clarendon Press, 1995, p. xii.

59. Müller, Harald, 'The Internalization of Principles, Norms and Rules by Governments', in V. Rittberger with P. Mayer (eds), *Regime Theory and International Relations*, 1995, p. 363.

60. Lister, Marjorie, *The European Community and the Developing World*, Aldershot, Avebury, 1988 and 1990, p. 133.

61. Haggard, Stephen, *Developing Nations and the Politics of Global Integration*, Washington D.C., Brookings Institution, 1995, p. 103.

62. Brigaldino, Glenn, 'Aid Effectiveness as a Multi-level Process', *D & C* (Development and Cooperation), DSE (Deutsche Stiftung für Internationale Entwicklung), Berlin, Issue 4/96, pp. 23–4.

63. Stokke, Olav, 'Aid and Political Conditionality' in Stokke, O. (ed.), *Aid and Political Conditionality*, London, Frank Cass, 1995, p. 13.

64. *Official Journal of the European Communities-C*, 24 November 1994, p. 431.

65. Development Assistance Committee of the OECD, 'European Community', 1996, p. 46.

66. *Ibid.*, p. 46.

67. Lingnau, Hildegard, 'Perspectives on Lomé Cooperation', Maastricht, European Centre for Development Policy Management Working Paper No. 12, May 1996, p. 5.

68. Singer, Hans, 'Aid Conditionality', Advanced Development Management Program, Series No. 13, Institute of Comparative Culture, Sophia University, Bulgaria, 1995.
69. *Ibid.*, pp. 18–19.
70. Development Assistance Committee of the OECD, 'European Community', 1996, p. 9.
71. IDS and IDR, *An Evaluation*, 1996, p. 41.
72. Development Assistance Committee of the OECD, 'European Community', Development Cooperation Review Series, No. 12, Paris, OECD, 1996.
73. *Ibid.*, p. 65.
74. *Ibid.*, p. 7.
75. Crawford, Gordon, 'Whither Lomé? The Mid-term Review and the Decline of Partnership', Paper to the Development Studies Association Annual Conference, University of Reading, UK, 18–20 September 1996, p. 22.

6 The African, Caribbean and Pacific Group of States' Experience of Partnership with the European Union

Carl B. Greenidge

THE NATURE OF THE ACP GROUP AND ITS SPECIAL CHARACTERISTICS

Trade dependence

The ACP states are a varied and polyglot group. That is well known. Less well known is the fact that these countries are for the most part unique in the extent to which they are trade dependent. The nature of the ACP's dependence on trade is of special significance at this juncture in time, given the arrangements evolving in relation to the international trade regime.

Commodity dependence

Commodities account for 70 per cent of the export earnings of the ACP states. Of the 25 low-income, severely indebted, exporters of non-fuel primary products, 21 are ACP states (IBRD, 1996). Additionally, 26 of the IBRD's 35 low-income commodity producers are ACP African states (IBRD, 1996). It is often contended that these characteristics of commodity dependence are not peculiar to the ACP Group and that comparable low-income countries should attract similar treatment to that which the EU provides to the ACP by way of trade cooperation. Bangladesh is frequently cited in this regard. And to be fair, Bangladesh is surely home to more poor persons than the ACP states, which together only account for 570 million souls. Unequal treatment of equals is unfair just as is equal treatment of unequals, so let us look at the indicators. We can do this with the aid of Table 6.1.

Table 6.1   Income status and trade dependence of ACP states relative
to three selected low-income Asian states

States	LDCs (UN classi- fication) X	Income category (high, medium and low)	Commodity* dependence as % of total export earnings (1992)	Market* con- centration for 3 main commodity X^3 (average 1989–91) (%)	Integration ratios (total exports/ GDP) (1993) (%)
Angola	X	M	95.0	95.0	76.6
Antigua and Barbuda		H	9.8	41.7	3.7
Bahamas		H	80.6	79.6	48.9
Barbados		H	37.8	41.7	11
Belize		M	75.8	58.4	21.9
Benin	X	L	93.8	83.7	2.3
Botswana		M	9.8	20.5	45.2
Burkina Faso	X	L	89.7	90.4	4.4
Burundi	X	L	87.1	91.0	7.2
Cameroun		M	98.2	69.9	15.3
Cape Verde	X	L	84.0	82.5	1.3
Central African Republic	X	L	37.6	49.5	8.9
Comoros	X	L	67.6	67.5	8.9
Congo		M	79.9	99.0	47
Côte d'voire		M	76.6	57.4	24.3
Djibouti	X	M	42.0	79.4	3.9
Dominica		M	62.8	57.3	29.1
Dominican Republic		M	90.5	69.1	5.4
Eritrea	X	L	–	–	na
Ethiopia	X	L	90.0	80.7	4.1
Fiji		M	65.8	52.4	24
Gabon		H	99.9	97.0	36
Gambia	X	L	15.9	30.8	18.7
Ghana		L	75.3	60.3	16.9
Grenada		M	58.2	54.2	13.5
Guinea	X	L	59.9	99.0	12.6
Guinea Bissau	X	L	99.9	80.9	6.6
Guinea Equatorial	X	L	88.5	62.9	39.5
Guyana		L	91.5	78.6	94.6
Haiti	X	L	22.7	22.1	3.7
Jamaica		M	83.6	64.7	27.8
Kenya		L	84.1	57.9	24
Kiribati	X	L	8.0	44.0	na
Lesotho	X	L	11.9	18.2	13.5
Liberia	X	L	41.7	76.2	22.7

Madagascar	X	L	79.8	45.0	7.8
Malawi	X	L	99.2	86.4	15.9
Mali	X	L	81.1	79.2	11.3
Mauritius		M	34.8	32.7	41.7
Mauritania	X	L	90.3	84.7	48
Mozambique	X	L	89.6	56.2	9.4
Namibia		M	61.2	22.8	52
Niger	X	L	99.5	96.7	11.3
Nigeria		L	99.9	99.7	40.2
Papua New Guinea		M	59.3	47.0	48.9
Rwanda	X	L	93.4	97.0	4
St Christopher & Nevis		M	48.1	43.0	16.9
St Lucia		M	64.9	83.2	25.2
St Vincent & Grenadines		M	82.8	77.5	29.8
Samoa	X	M	99.9	47.0	na
Sao Tome et Principe	X	L	61.3	76.0	12.8
Senegal		M	60.7	62.3	14.5
Seychelles		H	89.7	78.4	11.5
Sierra Leone	X	L	32.5	34.9	16.1
Solomon Islands	X	M	99.9	92.6	38.8
Somalia	X	L	18.4	83.4	na
Sudan	X	L	91.5	60.4	4.1
Suriname		M	99.0	88.8	83.3
Swaziland		M	64.5	36.5	59.6
Tanzania	X	L	64.8	54.5	16.9
Chad	X	L	53.5	67.2	11
Togo	X	L	56.8	71.7	23.2
Tonga		M	99.9	34.2	na
Trinidad and Tobago		H	70.6	67.6	35.5
Tuvalu	X	L	–	–	na
Uganda	X	M	99.9	93.1	4.9
Vanuatu	X	M	56.5	54.2	na
Zaire	X	L	99.9	82.4	4.3
Zambia	X	L	79.0	93.4	34.2
Zimbabwe		M	66.6	38.4	22.6
India		L	27.3	8.9	8.6
Pakistan		L	20.0	32.9	12.9
Bangladesh	X	L	18.4	36.9	9.4

* Including fuels.

For purposes of comparison we take the low-income states of India, Bangladesh and Pakistan, which although not 'typical' are often cited as deserving cases. We start with income distribution. Income levels are significant in the context of trade because low levels render economic actors less able to cope with fluctuations; and fluctuations there have been (see Greenidge, 1996).

The distribution of ACP states by income group is as follows:

- Low income   37
- Medium income   27
- High income   6

Most of the ACP states are in the low-income category. However, all three states, India, Bangladesh and Pakistan, in the reference group fall in this category. On these specific grounds therefore there appears to be a case for questioning the exclusiveness of the Lomé Convention.

On the other hand, when other relevant factors are taken into account most of the ACP states, including five classified as medium or middle income, may be placed among the globe's poorest or most disadvantaged. Thus the UN, utilising criteria based on a number of indicators not limited to income, classifies 39 ACP states as least developed (LLDCs).

In terms of commodity dependence, almost all ACP states are more dependent on commodity exports for foreign exchange than are India, Pakistan or Bangladesh. On the basis of 1992 figures, only 7 ACP states (excluding Tuvalu and Eritrea, for which no figures are available) are less dependent on commodity exports than the 3 Asian states. Whereas the latter's dependence ranges from 15 to 27 per cent, the ACP Group's commodity dependency is typically (21/70 states) 91–100 per cent. The dependence of some 16 states lies in the 75–90 per cent range, and altogether more than 60 ACP states have trade dependence such that their main commodity exports account for more than 30 per cent of total foreign-exchange earnings.

This is very significant when one recalls that over the years 1980–93, average commodity prices fell by 50 per cent in real terms. In 1993 alone this represented a total income loss of US$100bn to commodity exporters.

Market concentration

In addition to heavy dependence on commodity exports, states may depend inordinately on a single market. This is an important consideration in the context of liberalisation because it may limit the capacity to compensate across markets for competition in the main destination of exports. The modal concentration for ACP states is 91–100 per cent dependence on a single market for their 3 main commodity exports. In none of the three Asian reference states does that dependence exceed 37 per cent! ACP states are therefore not only characterised by commodity dependence but also heavy export market concentration.

By these measures of commodity and market concentration, only 10 to 13 per cent (9/66, 7/68) of ACP states can be considered remotely similar to the three Asian low-income states. The states which may be considered close to these three Asian economies include the Gambia, Haiti, Kiribati and Lesotho. It is difficult to imagine them having any other common characteristics! Using total exports to GDP as an indicator of integration, India, Bangladesh and Pakistan are 'less integrated' in the world economy than are most of the ACP states. This is an interesting comparison, since commentators frequently view the lack of ACP integration in the international trading economy as either the source or the reflection of their problems.

In terms of the structure of their economies, the difference between the three Asian states and the ACP are similarly very marked. Only Senegal, among ACP states, is classified as a low income, moderately indebted, *diversified* economy along with Bangladesh. None are found in the category with India and Pakistan as low-income, moderately indebted, *exporters of manufactures*.

It can be contended on the basis of these characteristics, therefore, that the ACP states are somewhat different from the other low-income states with which they are frequently compared. This means that changes in the trade regime are likely to affect them more significantly than these Asian states. The negotiators in the context of the GATT already recognised the necessity of making special allowance for LLDCs.

The question which therefore arises is whether the EU, in adjusting to the international climate by changing its trading arrangements and the system of Community Preference, should simply proceed on the assumption that *the consequences will be neutral across economies*. The ACP Group, as we have shown, is not an insignificant bloc of trade and EU-dependent states. Naturally, the Group would therefore wish to see appropriate arrangements in place before they agree to abandoning the regime of preferences. To date very little has been said about this aspect. And what has been said seems not to have attracted the serious attention it deserves.[1] After all, the euphoria about globalization, like that of the magic of the market, cannot hide the fact that these far-reaching changes do not automatically mean halcyon days for the weak and vulnerable. How, in terms of modalities and timing, do the EU and the WTO intend to handle the plight of the LLDCs, a plight recognised by all?

THE OBJECTIVES AND INSTRUMENTS OF THE LOMÉ CONVENTION

The stated objectives of the Convention have over the years been ACP-focused. Put briefly, the partners are seeking to deepen cooperation on a number of fronts and to enhance the social, economic and cultural situation of ACP countries by utilising trade instruments, technical cooperation and financial support. The trade instruments are employed on the basis of non-reciprocity and non-discrimination.

The parties' commitment to the overall objective of cooperation and development has remained unshaken over the five Conventions but the political conditionalities of the EU have sought to slant the mode of development increasingly in the image of Europe's wishes. The mid-term review added explicit EU objectives, namely those outlined in the Treaty of Maastricht, to the Convention. The importance of these trends is to be found in the preferred areas of cooperation and the pattern of aid – environment, sustainable forestry practices, good governance, and so on. The focus on decentralised cooperation is, similarly, consistent with a wish to see a much-reduced role for the state in keeping with Europe's ideological stance on development. However, the appropriate role of the state may be time-bound as well as spatially dependent. The capacity of the cooperant civic partners is also a variable which needs to be taken into account.

On the other hand, the ACP Group is not making much headway in changing or raising the tempo of cooperation in those areas which are of special interest to the Group. Among such areas are agriculture, fisheries, and processing, marketing, distribution and transportation (PMDT) as well as debt relief and investment flows.

In the meantime, the areas covered by the Convention are very extensive and the fact of the Commission's lack of enthusiasm for some areas and the Group's inability to access or meaningfully utilise others are giving rise to questions about whether Lomé is too comprehensive. Some observers have argued that this comprehensiveness and the consequential complexity are sources of confusion among potential beneficiaries.

It may also be the case that the human resources available in the ACP and Commission's bureaucracies for managing and monitoring the resources are not adequate, either in terms of their quality or their range. These are areas being highlighted from time to time but neither the Commission nor the General Secretariat are, in the current political and fiscal climate, in a position to argue their own cases persuasively. In the interim, the Commission is under pressure to keep costs down and to beef up the sections assigned to the preferred regions of Eastern Europe and the Mediterranean. Consequently, there are closures of Commission Delegation offices in some island states without so much as a murmur from those affected.

SOME ASPECTS OF THE EXPERIENCE OF PARTNERSHIP

Thwarted ambitions?

The developmental expectations of the various architects of the Conventions found under the label of Lomé were undoubtedly rather ambitious. However, the criticisms of the Convention and its effectiveness which enjoy wide currency frequently bear little relationship to those founders' intentions or hopes. It never crossed their minds that relatively limited levels of EU financial aid and of preferential access could alone in all circumstances lead to smooth and rapid development in all ACP states. Nor could they have reasonably anticipated the terms of trade decline suffered by the commodity producers in the 1980s and early 1990s. Yet in the press we find frequent reference to unqualified failure.

It is difficult to avoid the impression that much of this disenchantment and disappointment is attributable to advocacy, in many EU states, of simplistic panaceas which are informed by political considerations rather than technical and/or economic evidence. The position of ACP commentators has been not so much critical of cooperation itself as of the mode and sometimes intent of its management.

From a monitoring aspect, the management of some areas of cooperation has been a matter of concern because they have been increasingly bilateralised. Two cases in point are the fisheries agreements and National Indicative Programmes (NIPs). This leaves many ACP states thinking that they are securing special privileges from the EU whereas, had they been in a position to see what is taking place elsewhere, they may not have found this to be the case. It also leaves the Group as a whole in the dark about what is taking place in certain areas, especially as regards implementation.

Economic performance
- economic growth
- debt

- structural diversification
- trade

There seems to be a view current among European commentators that the poor performance of ACP states has contributed to aid fatigue in the EU. Before addressing the performance as such let us first recognise that this so-called aid fatigue – and Africa pessimism in particular – are reflections of a wider malaise with roots in the fiscal difficulties of member states and disillusion with the results of liberal politics in the post-Cold-War era.

A look at developments in other regions also attests to the fact that it is not merely the ACP or Africa with which the EU and OECD have difficulties. The most recent UNDP *Human Development Report* observes that the average per capita incomes of Latin America and the Maghreb states, *as well as those of sub-Saharan Africa*, have fallen since 1980. After a period of eulogising Asian states such as Vietnam, the Western press has started to be more critical of some of them as destinations for investment.[2] The source of the problem lies partly in the trademark of the press which involves finding a dramatic headline subsuming a simplistic idea and selling this to the public as a panacea.

The claims of pervasive poor performance of the ACP states are widespread enough not to warrant further repetition here.[3] Suffice it to note that half of Africa's 600 million populace lives in absolute poverty and, on the basis of current trends, it is the only region in which the number of poor will continue to increase until the year 2000. The late President of the World Bank (IBRD) noted that Africa receives US$4bn per annum in technical assistance and 100 000 accompanying experts, a larger number than existed at the time of independence.[4] At the same time, in Africa only Mauritius, Seychelles and Botswana rank above 100 in the UNDP Human Development Index. Actually, the performance of the ACP states has been mixed in relation to the general indicators on which a Convention such as Lomé can be expected to have a limited influence.

One of the main problems facing the ACP states is instability. Internal conflict is a major source of that instability. Indeed, this is not a problem peculiar to the ACP, for all of the 30 major armed conflicts of 1995 took place within national boundaries. In this regard, a recent survey of sub-Saharan Africa revealed that some ten states were devoting more to expenditure on defence and arms than they were on health. These states included Guinea Bissau, Chad, Burkina Faso, Zaire, Tanzania and Sudan.[5] Some widely publicised cases (such as Mozambique, Sierra Leone, Liberia?) are understandable and perhaps even 'justifiable' in some sense. But this cannot be true of all. Obviously, a considerable part of the responsibility for the plight of the ACP states can be laid at the door of their leadership and their approach to problems, internal and otherwise. At the same time it should not be forgotten that six of the world's top ten arms suppliers are EU member states with Germany and the UK heading the list, even as they publicly embrace second-generation conditionality. Clearly, the commitment to enforcing respect for human rights is only consistently pursued if it does not interfere with commercial interests. The recent events in Rwanda and Zaire lend credence to this depressing perception.

Slow economic growth obviously cannot be attributable to exceptional, external or special circumstances in all cases. Attempts to explain the difference in growth rates between Africa and comparable regions of the developing world have yielded some interesting results. Sachs has attributed somewhere in the region of 11 per cent of the difference to adverse structural factors such as lack of market access (landlocked countries, for example) and resource dependence.[6] But the two main explanatory factors were the relatively low savings rate and relatively low levels of openness. Additionally, the level of market efficiency also accounted for a significant proportion of the difference. Altogether, these factors explained some 90 per cent of the observed difference between Africa and comparable regions (Sachs, 1996).

It needs to be emphasized that several states in sub-Saharan Africa, the Pacific and the Caribbean have consistently pursued sound economic policies and have not had to resort to IMF medicine. The Pacific members of the Group, for example, have traditionally not encountered the kinds of problems mentioned above. The development of this region has traditionally been captive to geographical isolation, rapid population growth relative to the economy's capacity to absorb labour into the monetised economy, and natural disasters such as cyclones, earthquakes and drought.[7] Economic management has been traditionally very conservative. This – together with an open trading regime and relatively high levels of aid – has resulted in a stable financial environment, a sound balance-of-payments situation and stable exchange rates.

Over the years 1990 to 1994 most of the Pacific states have experienced positive GDP growth. The exceptions have been Kiribati and Samoa. Lately, fiscal deterioration, restricted possibilities for emigration, environmental degradation and changing relationships with their main donors have given rise to problems. At the same time, threats of political secession by elements in Bougainville, Papua New Guinea, and the constitutional problems in Fiji have adversely affected investment and development prospects. In Solomon Islands and Vanuatu, unstable co-alitions in government have probably had the same effect. These problems have been reflected in a weakening in the international reserve position of many states, including Fiji, Papua New Guinea (PNG), Samoa and Solomon Islands. In PNG's case the Kina has had to be floated. In the last analysis, like the remainder of the ACP Group, their future prosperity depends also on raising the currently low levels of savings and additionally on addressing the complex problems of land tenure reform.

In those ACP states which have encountered difficulties, a great deal is being done to meet the challenges of development. Frequently, they get little credit for these measures, which are universally harsh. At August 1996, for instance, ACP states were prominent among those undertaking the highest tranche adjustment programmes of the Bretton Woods institutions. The ratio of ACP states in total IMF Programmes was:

- 3/22 Standby Arrangements
- 1/10 Extended Fund Facility (EFF)
- 1/1 Structural Adjustment Funds (SAF)
- 20/29 Enhanced Structural Adjustment Facility (ESAF)

It needs to be noted that these often-harsh programmes have been willingly adopted, notwithstanding the equally severe criticisms of Structural Adjustment Programmes in general. Sachs, for example, has described them as being deeply flawed and unduly influenced by the IMF's obsession with price stability and the IBRD's lack of priorities. In support of his point he cites the case of Kenya, the Policy Framework Paper for which contained 111 conditions! Oxfam has been similarly critical.

Evidence of economic progress in the ACP states is available even in the regions commonly under the most severe stress. In 1990 there were in Africa 20 states with positive GDP growth. By 1996 there were over 40. Some, such as Botswana, Mauritius, Mozambique (after 1985), Namibia and the Seychelles, have entered exceptionally good performances over the period 1975–95. Others worthy of mention are Burkina Faso, Benin, Kenya and Lesotho (IBRD, 1996). Benin, the Gambia, Mali and Uganda are among countries which achieved growth rates which have been double that of the average for the rest of the region, tripled output in the critical agricultural sector and reversed the decline in exports (*Financial Times*, 27 September 1993).

When so many states have made an effort to put their economies in order it is especially disheartening to see official development assistance

(ODA) reduced, perhaps below the minimum level necessary to assist with the critical levels of public sector investment, especially in education and health.

Indebtedness

The EU was not at all inclined to discuss ACP indebtedness to member states during the course of the mid-term review. The ACP Group has argued that there is a case for a special effort by the EU to assist the ACP on this front (Greenidge, 1996). First, this is because the EU together with the multilateral financial institutions (MFIs) are the main creditors to the Group. Secondly, 18 ACP states are among the 20 most severely indebted states. To borrow the language of Professor Sachs (1996), in the light of the experience with Germany, Indonesia, Poland and Egypt, debt relief should be 'deep, phased over time and conditional on fundamental reforms'. One might add that in view of the impact of fiscal restraint in the context of structural adjustment programmes on the conditions of the poor, debt relief seems to be the most effective means of delivering meaningful and swift relief to the poor.

Trade cooperation

Export competitiveness

Basically, trade has not turned out to be the engine of growth that the ACP states had hoped. They are particularly unhappy about what appear to be inexorable declines in their share of EU imports. The EU has attributed this problem to the lack of competitiveness of ACP commodities. However, the most important of the causes has been the fall in commodity prices mentioned earlier, as well as:

- problems of access; and
- inadequate or non-existent levels of preference.

In any case, the widely accepted dismal picture on the trade front, to which the ACP has itself generally contributed, needs to be taken with a pinch of salt, or at least viewed more discerningly.

In the early 1990s some 26 ACP states enjoyed higher levels of export growth than the average for the Mediterranean and Latin America, while the performance of another eight exceeded the Asian average. This performance reflected success in a number of areas, including an expansion of new manufactures as well as of non-traditional exports of agricultural and horticultural products (ERO, 1996).

Even in the case of Africa the gloom is exaggerated. One needs, given the diverse nature of the continent, to go beyond the aggregate figures. In per capita export terms, Africa's performance (US$49.1 per capita), although not as good as would have been hoped, is on a par with that of Asia (US$51.2). Some states have experienced exceptional perform-ance. Gabon, Congo, Zimbabwe and Mauritius have been singled out in a recent study in this context. In the case of Mauritius, with a per-capita export level of US$941.06, its performance even exceeds that of Thai-land and Sri Lanka (US$449 and US$115.4 respectively) (Farqui *et al.*, 1996).

Africa is still improving on this export performance. Thus the IBRD's short-term projections indicated that sub-Saharan Africa experienced export growth of 10 per cent pa in 1995. For the fastest-growing states (15.9 per cent) and the Central African Franc (CFA) states exports ex-panded at 14 per cent, which is the same rate as East Asia (IBRD, 1996; pp. 22–3).[8]

The determinants of export competitiveness are of course many and account has to be taken of the negative impact of external shocks includ-ing political and military conflicts which were mentioned. In a recent comparison of the performance of Asia and Africa, the authors conclude that the most influential factor is the capacity of the individual manufac-turing firm. That capacity is in turn a function of incentive policies and supply-side factors. In examining the macro-economic factors they ob-served that most of the necessary changes have been made since, over the study period, there had been higher depreciation of the real exchange rate in Africa than had been experienced in Asia. But the dif-ference in economic performance of the two continents seems to be at-tributable to higher levels of technological effort, foreign investment, education and physical infrastructure (Farqui *et al.*, 1996). The Conven-tion needs to take account of these findings which are not very dissimilar to those of Sachs.

WTO-induced changes

Much is usually made of the claim that 97 per cent of all ACP products enter the EU duty-free. In reality, actual access for the ACP is not much better than that for the rest of the world for most exports. Some 63 per cent of ACP products enjoy no preferential margin at all, as may be seen below (ERO, 1996):

% of exports to the EU	Preferential margin over competitors
63	0
30	0-4.9
7	5

One of the main agreements under the new international trading regime is the tariffication exercise. This is expected further to reduce the level of preference enjoyed by the ACP Group in the context of Lomé. One author has argued that the impact of this exercise has so far been muted in the EU market because high internal and external prices during the base or reference period, 1986–8,[9] have meant on the one hand, high replacement tariffs, but on the other hand[10] there is still a minimum import price for other products.[11] The main problems therefore lie ahead.

Another major event lying in wait and likely to have a significant impact on the ACP–EU trade regime is the impending entry of Eastern and Central European states to the Union. Such entry, whether in the year 2000 or later, is likely to have consequences similar to those encountered with the entry of Spain and Portugal in 1989. In 1989 their incorporation into the system of Community Preference, which covers the Common Agricultural Policy (CAP), contributed to some trade diversion, especially in the case of sugar.

The problem of preferential access and of reciprocity

Special commodity protocols and the agreements covering temperate and horticultural products account for some 12.6 per cent of ACP exports to the EU. But the significance of these protocols to individual economies varies enormously, as may be seen below:

% of total exports to the EU	No. of ACP states
> 70	6
69.9–40	5
39.9–10	4
9.9–0	11
12.6	70 (% of total ACP – not including South Africa)

Over 70 per cent of some states' total exports to the EU consist of commodities covered by protocols and special agreements.

There is not the same degree of dependence or interest on the part of the EU. The EU's dependence on the ACP as suppliers has declined since 1975 but it still remains important in certain areas. A perusal of the main commodities traded between the EU and the Group shows that in

1994 the EU depended on the ACP to the following extent in the commodities named:

Commodity	% of EU imports accounted for by the ACP
sugar	78
coffee	29
petroleum	11
bananas	24
cocoa	87
chemical products	7
diamonds	18
aluminium	5

This suggests that the EU should still have an interest in the conditions likely to affect the capacity of certain ACP states to supply raw materials. On those grounds at least, it may be expected to continue to pay special attention to the protocols for sugar and to a lesser extent bananas.

The threat to the protocols from the World Trade Organisation (WTO) varies. The one likely to be under the least threat in terms of its existence is sugar, the life of which is indefinite. However, 'there is more than one way to skin a cat'. Although the existence of the sugar protocol as such is not under threat (unless the Convention itself is scrapped) there are other risks. Most prominent among these is the likely price squeeze, especially after the year 2005. In those circumstances the main onus is on the ACP producers to look carefully at complementary measures which include:

- enhancing the value added of their product by investment in facilities to enable production of white sugar or special niche-market sugars, such as Demerara and granulated. Indeed, in this regard the evolving technological changes in the industry have had the effect of enabling raw sugars to be substituted for whites.
- developing by-products of cane juice and the cane plant including bagasse-based by-products, and anhydrous ethanol fuel.

On the question of **non-reciprocity**, the EU's intentions are relatively clear. A model by way of South Africa exists alongside the drive to free trade agreements (FTAs) with each of the main regions in the rest of the world. These initiatives are likely to pose problems for the ACP because in order to be WTO-compatible they will in future not be able to exclude agriculture, or any other major area of trade between the partners for that matter. But agreements can be made over specific sensitive products. Such agreements will have implications for other countries (Fennell, 1996).

The challenge will be to balance all these, frequently conflicting interests, without further adversely affecting the position of the already genuinely disadvantaged. In this context the ACP may wish to urge the EU wholeheartedly to support and adopt the WTO's proposal that tariffs and non-tariff barriers be abolished on a range of exports of interest to the poorest countries, as a matter of highest priority.

Price and income instability

An exposé of the ACP's experience with trade cooperation has been analysed elsewhere. Here, I simply wish to touch on a neglected aspect which will have important implications for the future as structural adjustment programmes become more entrenched. By and large, under the dirigiste policies the price risk in agriculture was borne by the Marketing Boards or the Treasuries. Abolition of such entities is now in vogue. Thus, of the 51 International Coffee Organisation (ICO) members in 1985, 25 had Marketing Boards. In 1993 that number of Boards had been compressed to three. The problems for the farmers are becoming evident in economies with low per-capita levels of farmers' incomes and an associated restricted access to credit.

The plight of producers is made doubly hazardous by commodity markets, notorious for their volatility. High volatility with low prices and low credit is a recipe for problems. As observed earlier, commodity prices halved in real terms between 1980 and 1993. This was followed in some cases, such as base metals, cotton and rubber, by a steep price rise within a year – copper 70 per cent and aluminium 80 per cent, for instance. More recently, developments in these markets have given rise to further concerns about the lack of transparency in commodity exchanges and the impact of the latter on price volatility. Some banks which control as much as 75 per cent of stocks on the London Metal Exchange, for example, view them as profitable means of diversification from conventional securities. Similarly, US investment banks have been marketing them as a worthwhile non-inflationary diversion from bonds. In a not unrelated vein, a recent paper on the sugar market cited concerns over short-term manipulation by trading houses and investment funds as well as non-deliverability (UNCTAD, 1996).

Ever since organised markets were established commentators have worried about the likelihood of their being manipulated or of their being the object of speculation. The common response has been to deny the effect of speculation on commodity markets. A recent study of the impact of these tendencies and the impact of hedge funds and institutional investors in the case of cocoa concluded that such activities are unlikely to have any **sustained** effect on prices: a standard response. The author continues however, that this finding 'does not preclude the possibility that it does exaggerate short-term movements' (Gilbert, 1994). Since then, we have been treated to the Barings case and the equally spectacular case of the so-called 'Mr Five Percent', the technical trader of Sumitomo whose futile attempts to dictate market prices resulted in losses to the company of some US$2.6bn. The trader has since been accused of manipulating the market and of concocting fictitious trades with the aid of derivatives transactions and control of stocks on the London Metal Exchange. The revelation of the fraud led to a 30 per cent fall in copper prices.

Assistance is needed to meet this very debilitating economic phenomenon of instability. But, entities of EU member states are major players in such markets and the question that arises is whether member states can resist the temptation to hide behind claims about impartial and impersonal markets whilst their middlemen and consumers benefit from the misery of ACP commodity producers.

In the context of the Convention, the main instruments aimed at attenuating the impact of price and income volatility – Stabex and Sysmin – do not adequately serve these ends. The causes of this inadequacy are the paucity of resources for compensation relative to the price volatility on the one hand, and the tardiness with which the resources are disbursed on the other. In the face of EU unwillingness to address the problem of the adequacy of resources there has been growing attention paid to the possibility of using (by farmers) risk instruments. Such instruments are a means of protecting consumers and/or producers from price fluctuations without throwing all the burden of that protection on the Treasury. The instruments include:

- futures contracts;
- options;
- swaps; and
- new instruments such as deliverable forwards (*Aproma Review*, No. 50, 1996).[12]

One constraint on the ACP adoption of such instruments is the limited links between domestic producers/distributors and international export-

ers and or secondary markets. Assuming that the problem of small, fragmented and frequently uninformed producers in complex markets and
complicated market instruments can be overcome, the utility of these
instruments would be dependent on a number of factors which mainly
relate to legal and regulatory framework. More particularly:

- the availability of credit and therefore the financial system, tenure
  and property rights;
- tax and foreign exchange reforms in the states; and
- close technical supervision to handle speculation.

A recent study commissioned by the Group has recommended that the
ACP seek credit guarantees for the commodity exporters as a means of
facilitating the uptake of these instruments (WRI, 1996).

The European Development Fund (EDF): the financial envelope and capital flows

There are many influences bearing on the availability and use of financial resources for development. This is true of the global resource flows
as well as EU flows. In the recent past, practically all (97 per cent) the
financial flows reaching the ACP Group have taken the form of Development Assistance Committee (DAC) official assistance. The bulk of
those resources has come from the EU and its member states. Like the
rest of the OECD member countries, the EU member states seem unin-
clined to utilise whatever post-Cold-War peace dividend materialises for
the enhancement of development aid. An IBRD report concluded that,

> the prospects for ODA flows are not encouraging and there is little
> expectation that they will increase in real terms in 1996. All indications
> are that the flows of official development finance to low and middle in-
> come countries will fall in 1996 and beyond. (IBRD, 1996, p. 7)

This pressure on resources is compounded by the ideological preference
for channelling more and more resources through other civic partners –
under the aegis of decentralised cooperation.

For the world as a whole, total direct foreign investment (FDI) in 1995
was US$315bn, representing a 15 per cent increase over the levels of the
previous year. FDI has now become the principal element in private capital flows to LDCs. In 1995 the flow to developing countries stood at
US$100bn, compared with US$22bn of portfolio investment. 27 per cent

of FDI went to Latin America and two-thirds of this was directed to Mexico, Brazil, Argentina and Chile.

As with the LDCs, so it has been with the ACP. Private capital flows have reached the ACP Group essentially by way of FDI. However, unlike Latin America and Asia, FDI to Africa is low and has stagnated at US$5bn (UNCTAD, 1996) after a peak in 1989/91.

EU FDI flows to LDCs as a whole fell by more than half between the years 1991 and 1994, at which point they stood at ECU6.8bn (European Commission, 1995). The EU provides over 70 per cent of the investment from developed countries direct to the ACP. This FDI from the EU has tended to be clustered round the offshore banking, oil, and mining sectors and concentrated on a few countries, including those with large and growing markets. The main EU destinations have been:

- Nigeria
- Gabon
- Zimbabwe
- Côte d'Ivoire
- The Bahamas

The 1990s were expected to be the decade of equity investment. Whereas developing countries account for 13 per cent of the world's GNP they only have 6 per cent of world stock market capitalisation. It is necessary to exploit the much under-utilised potential of stock markets as a source of funds.

Improved macro-economic performance and structural diversification may help to make equity investment in Africa a more attractive prospect in the future. Of these, diversification is perhaps the most important factor for the inordinate dependence on commodity prices, the erratic nature of which is a much under-rated deterrent. Additionally, the rehabilitation of the Republic of South Africa is an important factor. Given its size, the Johannesburg Stock Exchange (JSE) is likely to be in a position to attract investors to the remainder of the continent if the Republic can overcome its own problems.[13]

The search for diversification by pension and other institutional funds mentioned earlier is leading managers increasingly to the doors of emerging markets in LDCs, including the ACP.[14] The allocation to such markets rose 5-fold between 1990 and 1994. So there is a large potential here and there is much that the EU can do to assist in the establishment of an appropriate environment by way of assistance with technical management and a regulatory framework.[15]

Some ACP states in Africa already enjoy good standing on the international capital markets, primarily on the basis of good performance and stability. Sovereign risk lenders' credit ratings show Botswana, Seychelles and Mauritius have a good standing, as do Ghana and Swaziland (Table 6.2). In the year 1992–3, the ratings of some 24 African countries improved whilst four declined.

There is a suspicion that the attention directed to Lomé in the context of the second generation conditionalities is attributable to the poverty of these countries and their limited countervailing commercial power. Corruption has been a major point of debate among commentators on the nature of development policies. Corruption is not a peculiarity of LDCs, of the ACP states, or indeed of the poor.

This suspicion is reinforced by the approach of the OECD countries to the phenomenon. Rightly much publicity is given to various initiatives such as that of the establishment of Transparency International and the recent signing by the Organisation of American States of a convention against corruption. But for all the acknowledgements that a moral and legal solution lies in addressing both bribers and recipients, the actions in the OECD countries are feeble and leave the onus and stigma on the poor countries: witness for example the fanfare surrounding the suit filed by the US Securities and Exchange Commission against Montedisson SpA over US$400mn of bribes they paid out between 1988 and 1992. The action, it is interesting to note, was merely a civil suit and was not in response to bribery *per se* but *in respect of accounting arrangements which had distorted the company's financial statements*.

Whilst we are on the question of corruption, it is most interesting to observe the recent furore over the funding of election campaigns in the US, in connection with which it has been estimated that US$1bn has been spent on the 1996 elections and another US$0.8bn is likely to be spent on the Senate elections. At the same time the role of special groups in this process should not be overlooked. Political power is bought and sold in the US. One commentator has described it thus, '[given] the take-over of politics by TV, political conduct is dominated by the necessity to conform to the demands of what is primarily a system of commercial entertainment' (*International Herald Tribune*). The US's entertainment is, however, less than amusing for the ACP because the 'payoff' of those very interest groups whose contributions were the subject of the headlines may create problems for the ACP in the future.[16] It should not be necessary to mention bananas or sugar to make the point.

Table 6.2   Institutional Investor's credit ratings for ACP states and other selected states including Bangladesh, India, Pakistan and South Africa

State	Global rank (1993)	State	Global rank (1993)
Angola	109	Mali	n/a
Antigua and Barbuda	n/a	Mauritius	51
Bahamas	n/a	Mauritania	n/a
Barbados	52	Mozambique	117
Belize	n/a	Namibia	n/a
Benin	n/a	Niger	n/a
Botswana	44	Nigeria	86
Burkina Faso	n/a	Papua New Guinea	54
Burundi	n/a	Rwanda	n/a
Cameroon	79	St Christopher-Nevis	n/a
Cape Verde	n/a	St Lucia	n/a
Central African Republic	n/a	St Vincent & Grenadines	n/a
Chad	n/a	Samoa	n/a
Comores	n/a	São Tomé & Príncipe	n/a
Congo	103	Senegal	88
Côte d'Ivoire	99	Seychelles	84
Djibouti	n/a	Sierra Leone	126
Dominica	n/a	Solomon Islands	n/a
Dominican Republic	94	Somalia	n/a
Eritrea	n/a	Sudan	125
Ethiopia	n/a	Sudan	n/a
Fiji	n/a	Suriname	77
Gabon	63	Swaziland	110
Gambia	n/a	Tanzania	n/a
Ghana	74	Togo	n/a
Grenada	124	Tonga	59
Guinea	n/a	Trinidad and Tobago	n/a
Guinea Bissau	n/a		
Guinea Equatorial	n/a	Tuvalu	121
Guyana	n/a	Uganda	n/a
Haiti	122	Zaire	115
Jamaica	78	Zambia	112
Kenya	72	Zimbabwe	66
Kiribati	n/a		
Lesotho	n/a	Bangladesh	90
Liberia	127	India	49
Madagascar	n/a	Pakistan	60
Malawi	100	South Africa	45

CHALLENGES TO THE PARTNERSHIP

The role of the ACP states and the agents of the ACP and Commission

Partnership is a strongly entrenched feature of the Convention. It is reflected at a number of levels. Perhaps it is most highly valued in so far as it applies to the workings of the joint institutions. The value of a standing platform for consultation, negotiation, complaints and dialogue cannot be exaggerated in the context of current international relations where LDCs and their preferences count for very little.

Nevertheless there is a limit to partnership, especially when one partner has an obligation to provide finances. In such cases, rules for resolving disagreements between the partners cannot, in most instances, be quite so egalitarian. In the invoking of the suspension clause and the resolution of disagreement over the aid envelope and trade chapters, for example, one encounters the principle of 'he who pays the piper...' Or, as William Cobbett so cogently put it in his 'Advice to Young Men', 'to be poor and independent is very nearly an impossibility'.

The changing roles of the political fora such as the Joint Assembly, Council of Ministers, ECOSOC and Chambers of Commerce

Over the last few years the Council of Ministers seems to have declined as a forum for structured political exchanges between the two partners. This has been the case even as other regions without such a special relationship with the EU have had their ministerial consultations elevated to standing fora for effective political dialogue. Part of the problem may lie in the structuring of the dialogue and the fact that the traditional ACP ministers are neither fish nor fowl, that is, neither responsible for foreign affairs nor for trade. This provides these ministers opposed to debating controversial matters in this regard with the handy excuse of not having been briefed beforehand by their colleagues responsible for foreign affairs. This has been reinforced by the inability or unwillingness of the ACP Council and the Committee of Ambassadors formally to criticise or chastise members of their group in cases of failure to respect mutually agreed rules. The problem here is that they are government representatives.

In other words, the demonstrated weaknesses of these fora may reinforce another tendency of the EU anyway and that pertains to the role of the state. In EU member states politicians and governments are the subject of a great deal of disenchantment. The EU and their member states in turn regard ACP governments in an even worse light than they themselves are regarded by their constituents. Sometimes to hear it told, corruption is a unique feature of ACP or LDC governments. As one commentator was driven to observe, 'elected governments are considered less trustworthy than pop singers that no-one voted for'.[17] Perverse though it may seem therefore this approach, given the availability of resources and capacities, makes it difficult to avoid the impression that foreign NGOs (as opposed to Governments or Southern NGOs) appear to be preferred by the EU as partners. This is one sense in which the partnership is changing both qualitatively and by way of the actors. It is likely that this approach will in time lead to pressure to modify the central role played by the government and ambassadors in the negotiations and in the monitoring of the implementation of the Conventions.

But just as the Ministerial forum seems to be declining as a structured platform for political dialogue between the ACP and EU, the Joint Assembly has come into its own. Especially for the reasons provided above, it can be expected that the EU will find a means of encouraging the non-government fora, such as the Joint Assembly and the Economic and Social Committee, to be more assertive.

The NGOs have played a very important role in development aid. In the current context they have contributed enormously to securing and maintaining public support for aid, especially in the context of emergencies. However, the fad by which they are touted as remedies for corrupt behaviour or state incompetence in LDCs is cause for concern. NGOs are themselves encountering problems in this area. Recent research on NGOs, for example, points to the many 'slips between the cup and the lip'.[18] These arise from an unholy rush to direct resources to this politically 'sexy' area oblivious of their limited capacities.[19] As a consequence, in the ACP states, as elsewhere in the LDCs, there is a degree of tension arising from the operations of NGOs because some are seen, *inter alia*, as foreign quangos in disguise, which both decide and implement what should be Government policy.[20] There are also problems arising from the operations of tele-evangelists and philanthropist entrepreneurs, and from the support which is provided, unintentionally or otherwise, to 'unworthy' beneficiaries. These difficulties have reached their greatest peak to date in the case of Rwanda. In reaction to these experiences there have been calls for a 'code of conduct' for NGOs. This is something which the ACP may wish to take up also.

As observed elsewhere, the real problem with which the development agencies have to grapple is how to bridge the gap between operational realities on the one hand and what may be laudable concepts or ideas on the other. It is necessary to be more critical in approaching these initiatives. There are no panaceas in development, neither anti-corruption drives nor NGOs.

The problems of human rights, good governance and democracy are only effectively tackled at political fora. The partial approach of the EU to human rights has yet to be forcefully adressed by the ACP side and indeed they have yet to develop an acceptable approach to formulating an ACP position. Constitutions and political practices in the ACP are supposed to deal with civil and political liberties but what is to become of economic and social rights, the absence of which may undermine political stability? What *quid pro quo* should the ACP extract? Can they insist that aid and Bretton Woods structural adjustment programmes be packaged to support economic and social rights meaningfully? In that case what will they be saying about military aid? The other problem is which of these goals will the EU be willing to forgo when the achievement of all of them turns out to be contradictory? Often the commercial interests of the EU are treated as sacrosanct, so good governance and respect for human rights have to take a back seat to the economic interests of member states.[21]

CONCLUSION

The objectives of a new Convention will have to be modified to reflect economic and political realities. These realities may well not require as radical a change in the Lomé Convention as is commonly claimed. In any case, for the ACP, undoubtedly the greatest threat is posed by the changes in the trading regime, not only in terms of the intended changes but also the likely results. Many of the other proposed changes will involve problems in so far as it may not be easy to fashion working means that can really enable the achievement of goals that may be more idealistic than practical.

Notes

1.　See, for example, the proposal (mentioned later) from Mr Ruggiero of the WTO, a proposal which seems so far not to have found favour with the US.
2.　See for example *International Herald Tribune*, 19 November, where, in an article entitled 'Now Disenchantment with Vietnam', political ambivalence, capricious decisions and widespread corruption are cited.

3.   For an outline of some of the more problematic indicators, see Greenidge, 1996.
4.   *The Financial Times*, 27 September 1993. Oxfam has also made this point.
5.   *The Economist*, 7 September 1996, 'Sub-Saharan Survey', p. 17.
6.   15 states in Africa have no direct access to the sea.
7.   Not to mention coastal pollution, depleted inshore fisheries, damage to coral reefs, shortage of potable water and inadequate waste management.
8.   These were comprised of
     - Cameroon and the Congo – oil;
     - Ghana and Zimbabwe – metals and minerals;
     - Botswana, Uganda and Mauritius (also SA) – manufacturing;
     - Kenya and Malawi – horticulture.
9.   Of variable import levies, minimum import prices and voluntary export restraint.
10. Products, such as fruit and vegetables, are subject to a minimum import price combined with a tariff.
11. Meaning that there now exists privileged market access for exporters previously subject to quotas and export restraints.
12. Lest, in the light of the recent claims on Stabex (1984/year of application), one gets the impression that the problems that such instruments are intended to address are a thing of the past, it should be noted that the recent IBRD short-term commodity price projections suggest that the terms of trade will move against commodity producers again before 1998.
13. The JSE is several times larger than the average (US$20–60bn) emerging market, with capitalisation of US$105bn. Africa had, in 1994, only 12 liquid stocks with market capitalisation in excess of US$100mn and 7 of those were in Morocco.
14. Estimated at over US$5000bn currently.
15. Once the necessary basics are in place in terms of fiscal and monetary policies.
16. A Guyanese proverb most apt in this situations is that what is fun for little boys is death for a cockroach.
17. E. Mortimer, 'NGOs rule OK' and 'At Arms Length', *Financial Times*, 22 March 1985 and 21 September 1994 respectively.
18. See ODI reports on impact assessment of NGO operations, which question the impact of NGO projects at the project level.
19. Hence they take on more than they can manage. In Rwanda there were many coordination problems; several NGOs handle more cash, with none of the managerial safeguards, than many MNCs. They need a code of conduct with regard to certain ethics as regards dealings with governments, political issues, and relief operations being turned into business for personal and institutional gain, embroilment in local disputes over food aid distribution and pillaging etc.
20. Between a third and 35 per cent of the funds raised by US (US$bn) and British (US$0.5bn) NGOs in 1994 originated with the respective governments. Indeed, the pressure of donors to have the NGOs pursue the short-term objectives of their donor governments more assiduously has been the source of NGO donor government conflict. See ODI (1995b).
21. Some insights into these issues are clearly provided by Crawford (1995).

References

Camdessus, M. (1996) 'African Prospects Tied to Courageous Adjustment Efforts'. Opening Remarks delivered at the Summit of Heads of State and Government of the OAU, in Yaounde, Cameroun, 9 July. Reproduced in *IMF Survey*, 29 July 1996.

Crawford, G. (1995) 'Promoting Democracy, Human Rights and Good Governance Through Development Aid: A comparative study of the policies of 4 Northern Donors'. University of Leeds, Centre for Democratization Strategies, Working Paper on Democratization.

ERO (1996a) 'ACP Experiences of the Lomé Trade Provisions. ACP–EU Trade Relations'. Section 2, ERO/ECDPM Information Pack.

ERO (1996b) 'The Significance of Lomé Trade Preferences for the BTNs and EU–South African Free Trade Area'. Brussels. October.

European Commission (1995) 'Draft Report on the Investment Flows Between the European Union and the ACP States'. DG for Development, Division of Industrial Cooperation. September.

Farqui, R. and Wignaranja, G. (1996) 'Can Africa compete in manufactures?' *International Capital Markets*, Vol. 16, No. 1, September. Commonwealth Secretariat, London.

Fennell, R. (1996) 'Community Preference and Developing Countries'. Conference paper, 'Europe and the Developing Countries Conference', 17 October, European Parliament Office, London.

Gilbert, C. (1994) Commodity Fund Activity and the World Cocoa Market. London Commodity,

Greenidge, Carl, B. (1996) 'Return to Colonialism? The new orientation of European Development Assistance'. Paper delivered to Association of German NGOs on the Occasion of their Annual General Assembly, Bonn, September.

IBRD (1996) 'Global Economic Prospects and the Developing Countries: short term update'. 29 August; IED, Development Economics, World Bank.

Nunnay-Elam, F. (1996) 'The Case for Risk Management in Emerging Countries'. World Commodity Report, Finance, 1 September.

ODI (1995a) 'The Impact of NGO Development Projects'. Briefing Paper No. 2, May, London.

ODI (1995b) 'NGOs and Official Donors'. Briefing Paper No. 4, August, London.

Sachs, J. (1996) 'Growth in Africa. It can be done!' *The Economist*, 29 June, pp. 2–25.

UNCTAD (1996) 'Prospects for the World Sugar Economy in the light of the Uruguay Round Agreements'. UNCTAD/COM/72, August.

Warwick Research Institute (1996) 'Commodity and Risk Management Policies for the 1990s'. A report submitted to the ACP Group of States.

7 Bureaucratic Interests and European Aid to Sub-Saharan Africa

Gorm Rye Olsen

F15   F35   O19

INTRODUCTION

There is a widespread consensus that international development aid has been under heavy pressure in recent years. A number of the big donors have made drastic cuts in their development aid budgets. This is not only true for the US; big European donors such as Germany and the UK have also decreased their development aid. Although the total nominal value of official development aid (ODA) appears to remain at a level of just below 60 billion US dollars per year in the mid 1990s, the real value of ODA is slowly being undermined. Thus from 1994 to 1995 ODA declined by almost 9 per cent due to inflation and currency values. In the OECD countries the decreasing political will to contribute to international development aid manifests itself in falling average aid measured as a percentage of GNP. The most recent figures show that the average ODA from the OECD countries was 0.27 per cent of GNP for 1995, down from 0.33 per cent in 1992 (OECD, 1997).

'Europe', specifically the 15 EU countries plus the EU Commission, disburses around half the total ODA. So how these 15 donors (Greece has no official aid programme) behave in disbursing aid is extremely pertinent. Since the European donors provide at least half the global ODA which goes to sub-Saharan Africa it is of the greatest importance to the countries in that region that Europe continues to allocate aid at least at the same volume as now. Of course, this assertion presupposes that Africa wants Europe to continue supporting the development efforts of the continent.

Thus, the basic question of this paper is: Is it possible to identify forces and circumstances (here called determinants) in Europe which will struggle to keep Africa on the European agenda and which in particular are willing to commit themselves to ensuring that Europe continues its considerable aid commitment to Africa? And can this commitment be maintained despite the insignificant economic, political and security interests Europe has in the continent? Furthermore, does there exist such a commitment despite the fact that Africa has become even less important to Europe after the end of the Cold War?

Determinants are, in what follows, defined rather broadly as values, perceptions and social groups (social forces) which are involved in policy-making processes related to aid. Hence, in principle, all individuals, organisations, institutions and political parties in Europe which articulate ideas or claims related to aid are relevant to the following discussion.

Ideally, the term 'European aid' in this paper should refer to Lomé aid plus the bilateral aid of the individual EU donors which have aid programmes. Thus we should cope with different actors, that is, the 14 bilateral donors and the European Commission in Brussels. However, due to lack of space and data, the paper only focuses on the bilateral determinants of three European donors in order to get a preliminary impression of the possible 'European' forces committed to Africa and to aid to Africa. Thus the determinants of common EU aid and the determinants of the 12 other bilateral donors will not be addressed here.

The paper deals specifically with Germany, Denmark and the UK. Germany is one of the most important powers in the post-Cold-War world and furthermore, measured in absolute figures, Germany is also one of the biggest aid donors. In relative terms, however, German ODA declined to 0.31 per cent of GNP in 1995. Denmark is a small country, but in development aid it is number one if measured by ODA as a percentage of GNP. Thus, in 1995, Denmark gave 0.96 per cent of its GNP in aid. Britain is chosen mainly because it is a former colonial power and is still considered a world power. In 1995, UK ODA in absolute figures fell behind that of the Netherlands, while relatively speaking aid was more or less on the international average, that is 0.28 per cent (OECD, 1997). The argument of this paper is to be sketched out as follows. First, there is a brief discussion of the possible determinants of European aid and a model is presented of a policy network of a bilateral European aid donor. There then follows a discussion of aid as a policy issue. After this ensues the analysis starting with Germany and succeeded by Denmark. Finally comes the analysis of the UK.

Determinants of European aid

Before embarking on the empirical analysis, it is necessary to identify the possible determinants of European development aid. It is obvious that the motives of the individual donors are important in this context. For most European donors there are already a number of empirical analyses

of aid motives which point in the direction of aid being primarily determined by donor interests and to a lesser extent by recipient needs (Bowles, 1989; Maizels and Nissanke, 1984). Recipient needs are especially
important in the case of smaller donors such as the Scandinavian states
and the Netherlands.

The motives of aid are closely linked to the kind of domestic political
values which are predominant in the individual donor countries. If these
values are institutionalised they are supposed to have an impact on the
aid policy which is pursued by a particular donor (Noël and Thérien,
1995; Stokke, 1989). These authors agree that domestic political values
are of particular importance in smaller states and that, possibly, this is
not the case for the bigger donors. However, in this paper it is assumed
that domestic values in general are gaining more and more influence in
foreign-policy making, including that of the bigger states of Europe.
Martin Shaw claims that it is characteristic that 'international relations
between states are increasingly about issues within societies' (Shaw,
1992, p. 426). And in the academic literature, it is generally accepted that
domestic circumstances including domestic values seem to be more and
more important in determining the foreign-policy behaviour of the
OECD states, not least after the end of the Cold War (Rosenau, 1992;
Kegley, 1992).

Here, it is suggested that domestic values are closely related to the notion that the decision makers in foreign aid (and in foreign policy) have a
relatively clear perception of the role their country should play in international politics (cf. Breuning, 1995). It can furthermore be argued that
the role perception is related to the idea of Steven Hook (1995) that
there is this close link between the national interest, however defined,
and the aid policy of a given country.

Based on the academic literature on aid, there is a solid foundation for
the assumption that policy making on aid largely takes place within a separate sector of each national European political system. In general, public policy in OECD countries is largely departmentalised and thus
differentiated along functional lines (Smith, 1993; Rhodes and March,
1992). This implies that the decision makers in aid policy are, to a large
extent, separated from the decision makers in other policy fields such as
agricultural policy, environmental policy and so on. As a consequence,
we also have to accept that the persons and institutions involved in decision making on general foreign policy issues may be separated from
those involved in aid.

In an attempt to specify the relevant decision makers involved in aid, it
is suggested that the concept 'policy network' is a useful tool, stressing

that such networks may vary from the very closed 'policy community' to the loose 'issue network'. It might be worthwhile to emphasise the basic assumption of the policy network approach, which is that the policy outcome (in this case European bilateral aid to Africa, primarily) depends on the type of relationship which exists between groups and state actors in this kind of activity. Furthermore, the outcome depends on the type of political values and the national interests which are predominant in the country in question. This implies that the pattern of policy making most probably differs between policy areas and, therefore, aid policy making is probably characterised by some specific features that are different from other areas. For the discussion in this paper, it further implies that the pattern of policy making might differ from one European bilateral donor to another.

In model 1, the actors assumed relevant in the policy networks of European bilateral aid are presented. It appears that when we focus on aid to Africa the NGOs, the media and public opinion are regarded as potentially important determinants along with the government, parliament and so on. The model also contains 'non-actor determinants' such as domestic political values which are considered possible determinants of aid. The same is true for the national interest/the national role perception which are more or less synonymous in the model. Therefore, the non-actor determinants are located in the model on an equal footing with the other so-called actor-determinants.

As to the international system as a possible determinant, the model narrows it down to the international donor community, for example, the World Bank. Also, the objective or structural conditions for foreign policy behaviour (cf. Carlsnaes, 1992) are included. It is assumed that the latter determinant has both a direct impact on the aid policy and an indirect one via the decision makers' perception of the current international location of their country.

The so-called 'non-actor determinants' in the model contain explanatory elements such as the possible significance of domestic values and the role perception of the relevant decision makers. However, we need to present assumptions about the relevant actors and their behaviour. Concerning political parties, parliaments and governments, one very important determinant of the behaviour of politicians is their wish to be elected and re-elected. Furthermore, this implies an assumption that European politicians, including government members, do not wish to present points of view which are distant from or at variance with the main attitudes of the electorate. The determination of the motives of the business community may be the least complicated, as its main interest is expected to be profit maximisation now and in the mid-term perspective.

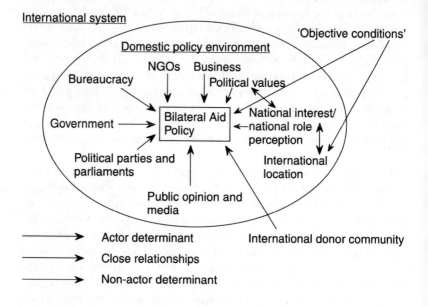

Figure 7.1   Policy network of a bilateral European aid donor

The interests of the bureaucracy may be determined by combining reflections from 'new institutionalism' with older ideas on 'bureaucratic politics' (March and Olsen, 1989). These lead to at least one basic assumption: namely that institutional interests and interests of individual bureaucrats are important determinants of institutional behaviour. The theories mentioned emphasise that interests are tied to the expansion of the areas of responsibility of the institution, the subsequent expansion of its budgets and thus the improvement of the career opportunities of the individual civil servants. At a minimum, bureaucratic interests consist in defending the size of the current budget and the current overall responsibilities of the institution.

Finally, there are the concerns of the NGOs. They are normally assumed to be driven by idealistic and moral motives such as a sense of 'global responsibility' (Shaw, 1992; Ghils, 1992; Lipschutz, 1992). However, I will argue that NGOs over a rather short time span tend to develop attitudes that are very similar to those of other large and bureaucratic organisations such as ministerial departments. Thus, the hypothesis

related to the interests of the NGOs is similar to that of the bureaucracies mentioned above.

The idea of applying the concept of policy networks to foreign aid is
not necessarily original. Morrissey, Smith and Horesh use, to some
extent, the same approach in their study of British aid policy. However,
the authors find that the concepts of 'withinsiders' who have direct input
to Whitehall decision-making and 'insiders' who only have direct access
to government are more fruitful concepts compared to the concept of
policy networks (Morrissey, Smith and Horesh, 1992, p. 58). McGillivray
and White (1993) appear to think along similar, though not identical,
lines to those followed here. Their thesis is that 'an aid allocation is the
outcome of a bureaucratic decision-making process, which is subject to
both bureaucratic criteria and the economic, political and other relations between donor and recipient' (*ibid.*, p. 68).

AID AS A POLICY ISSUE

However briefly, it is important to characterise aid as a specific policy
issue within the broader context of national politics in European countries. In Germany, Denmark and the UK, Africa, and thus aid to Africa,
is clearly a minor political issue within the overall political context of
these countries.

For German foreign policy, Africa is not a priority area. The priorities
lie elsewhere as the traditional focus of German foreign policy is still on
Western Europe with special emphasis on the intimate relationship to
France, followed by NATO, G-7 plus Eastern Europe and Asia (Rummel, 1996). 'Relations with Africa in all fields have a particularly low profile and are carried on largely as a matter of routine, but without any
sense of priority or overriding significance' (Hofmeier, 1984, p. 81).

In Denmark, development aid and relations to Africa are also of
minor significance. In the context of Danish foreign-policy priorities, the
European Union and NATO, including the transatlantic relationship,
have the highest priority. However, Denmark also gives considerable
priority to international cooperation including a strengthening of the
UN system and international development cooperation (Petersen,
1995). In this last context, it is a clear and official aim of Danish policy to
prioritise Africa. In 1994, there was a debate in the Danish parliament
which showed very broad support for working in favour of putting Africa
and its development problems both on the European and on the international agenda. The EU and the UN plus the World Bank and the IMF

were explicitly mentioned in the final resolution as the relevant bodies for ensuring international attention on Africa.

Africa, and the rest of the third world for that matter, are no doubt only marginal to British foreign-policy concerns, not to mention British policy concerns in general (Hill, 1996). As an illustration, aid represents a minor share of the budget with less than 1 per cent of public spending in the 1980s. Therefore it is legitimate to conclude that aid is not 'a major concern to taxpayers/voters but can be used to appease or reward interest groups and supporters' (Morrissey *et al.*, 1992, p. 2).

It is worth mentioning *en passant* that, when compared to Germany, Denmark and Great Britain, France represents a clear exception to the pattern of low profile. France is the only European country in which a strong national interest in Africa is explicitly formulated (Schraeder, 1995, pp. 541–5; Martin, 1995). We would hence expect that the determinants of French aid, the motives for keeping Africa on the agenda and putting priority on aid to the continent are very different from the three countries analysed below. However, France is not included in the analysis that follows.

GERMANY

Since the end of the Cold War, Africa south of the Sahara has been of marginal interest to united Germany. The economic, the security and other interests related to the continent of Africa are insignificant. Therefore, it seems legitimate to conclude as Stefan Mair does: 'Due to its economic significance to the African governments, development cooperation is no doubt the most important instrument of Germany's Africa policy' (Mair, 1996, p. 61).

The official aim of German aid (to Africa) was spelled out in 1975 as 'the improvement of the economic and social situation of people in developing countries and in developing their creative capabilities' (Nölke and Obser, 1994, p. 1). In spite of this official aim, during the Cold War there were also other motives underlying (West) Germany's policy towards Africa. First of all, Germany, along with its Western allies, tried to contain Soviet expansion on the continent. Following the Hallstein doctrine, development aid policy was specifically aimed at marginalizing the German Democratic Republic (GDR) in Africa.

Hence German development aid policy for many years has consisted of a mixture of different motives which can hardly be separated from each other. They include both humanitarian motives and support for

German economic self interest. But it 'definitely also [contains] a genuine development policy geared towards the attainment of long-term effects and in support of the emancipatory efforts of the developing countries' (Hofmeier and Schultz, 1984, p. 236). This assessment leads Nölke and Obser to conclude that 'compared to a number of other donor countries, German development aid has never been completely determined by narrow economic interests, but has been based on a mixture of economic, political and "developmental" motives' (Nölke and Obser, 1994, p. 6).

The end of the Cold War and the unification of the GDR and the Federal Republic of Germany (FRG) changed Germany's foreign policy interests *vis-à-vis* Africa. It also changed the perception of the German decision makers as to which role the new and unified Germany should play in world politics. In 1993, Chancellor Helmut Kohl made a speech making it clear that 'It is our duty as a rich nation also in the future to contribute to solutions to the pressing global problems. In this context, the emphasis of German policy is on: dialogue and smoothing out differences between North and South, demands for dynamic development, the fight against hunger, poverty and environmental degradation...' These broad remarks were later backed by a White Paper published by the German defense ministry (Mair, 1996, pp. 32–4).

The possibility that the so-called ethical or value policy of Germany in reality plays a role in policy towards sub-Saharan Africa is made probable by the insignificant economic interests of Bonn in Africa. Only around 1 per cent of German imports come from the region and the region only takes about 1 per cent of Germany's exports. South Africa and Nigeria are by far the most important African countries for German foreign trade. German direct investments in the continent are insignificant: 1 per cent of total net investments went to sub-Saharan Africa in 1994 compared to 2 per cent in 1980. Most investments are in South Africa.

To sum up what has been said so far, after the end of the Cold War, the motives of German aid may still be mixed, but if the focus is specifically on aid to Africa it is at least possible to fix an order of priorities of these motives. 'German Africa policy since 1990 is primarily determined by ethical interests (*Werteinteressen*) and weaker interests related to security, economy and power politics', Stefan Mair argues (Mair, 1996, p. 64).

The insignificant German economic interests lead Hofmeier to stress the point that 'due to the absence of other significant interests, the aid programme is in fact by far the most important dimension of bilateral relations between Germany and any given African country' (Hofmeier, 1994, p. 74).

Due to the marginal German interests in sub-Saharan Africa, there has been a long tradition – dating back to the years of the Cold War – for Bonn to accept the special role of France and her interests in Africa. Because the special relationship with France has been one of the most, not to say *the* most important determinant of German foreign policy, German governments have until very recently avoided any dispute or critical discussion with France over her African policies (Hofmeier, 1994, p. 78).

However, since the Rwanda tragedy in 1994, German Africa policy has become somewhat more reluctant to follow French policy in Africa. This change in policy is due to a widespread perception in German policy-making circles dealing with Africa that France's Africa policy is unpredictable. On the other hand, this new realisation has left the German position in a vacuum, implying that every new policy initiative towards Africa is now taken on an issue-by-issue basis.

Actors in German aid

Because Germany has no vital interests in sub-Saharan Africa,

> organised groups or indeed individuals may succeed in influencing German Africa policy in favour of their specific interests. Therefore, the limited general German interest means that long-term country policies are lacking and also, only ad hoc reactions to actual developments or crises are the result. (Mair, 1996, p. 66).

In spite of this, public support for development cooperation had always been relatively high in West Germany before unification and continues to be relatively high post unification. Thus in 1987, 75 per cent of the population approved of development assistance in general. In 1994, a new survey showed that a large majority of Germans take an interest in development cooperation. The great majority of the population – 75 per cent in the West and 69 per cent in the East – indicated that they were in favour of development cooperation. About one-fifth of both West and East Germans expressed a strong or very strong interest in issues of development policy and they indicated that they were willing to make a personal contribution (Wiemann, 1997).

On the other hand, development issues rank below domestic issues in the public's perception (Wiemann, 1997). This seems to be in line with Hofmeier's conclusion: 'aid is obviously still not a particularly popular subject. Deep-rooted scepticism about the practical effects of aid programmes remains' (Hofmeier, 1994, p. 77). Thus, it is not surprising that development aid in general and aid to Africa in particular are not important political issues in German politics.

Moreover, since the end of apartheid in South Africa, aid to the continent is not a topic of particular controversy in the German Bundestag. This is partly due to the widespread consensus with respect to the declared general principles underlying German development policy. The infrequent controversies over aid and Africa in general are mostly related to specific cases (like the human rights situation in Nigeria). Only a handful of politicians in parliament take a real interest in development issues, including African affairs. This is explained by the total lack of a political constituency for Africa in Germany and also by the fact that none of the political parties have a specific concept or an idea for an African policy (Hofmeier, 1994, p. 80).

The parliament's Committee of Development Cooperation (*Ausschuss für wirtschaftliche Zusammenarbeit*, AWZ) has some influence on German aid and on African policy in general. It is partly exerted via the organisation of hearings on special issues. Some observers suggest that the AWZ may be considered as a lobby group working in favour of aid, but on the other hand the same observers characterise the influence of the committee as weak.

The federal administrative organisation with responsibility for aid to Africa is complicated as a number of ministries and more or less independent organisations are involved in forming and executing German policies. Policies at the central or federal level are determined by at least three ministries with overlapping responsibilities and to some degree with divergent views and interests. The situation is further aggravated by the fact that German ministers tend to act on their own and without any real coordination with the other relevant ministries.

The organisational structure is also characterised by a separation between the policy-making level and the level of policy implementation. The Ministry of Development Cooperation, the BMZ, is supposed to be the centre of the organisations as it is the main institution responsible for aid policies towards Africa including planning, aid principles, programmes and the overall coordination of German bilateral aid cooperation. In formal terms, the BMZ is secondary to the Ministry of Foreign Affairs. But normally, the BMZ formulates German aid policy which is then subsequently delegated to a second level consisting of representatives of independent public implementing agencies such as Kreditanstalt für Wiederaufbau (KFW), Gesellschaft für Technische Zusammenarbeit (GTZ) plus NGOs, including the political foundations attached to the major political parties (Nölke and Obser, 1994, pp. 6–7).

However, the German Ministry of Foreign Affairs has a strong say in the inter-departmental discussions which are involved whenever the BMZ proposes a policy which might be detrimental to French interests. In such cases it may lead to pressure from the Ministry of Foreign Affairs on the BMZ to change its policy. Recently, debt relief to former French colonies in West Africa can be mentioned as an example, where the Ministry of Foreign Affairs has pressured the BMZ to change its original proposal for a German policy on the subject. On the other hand, the Ministry of Foreign Affairs accepted the so-called 'Accra principles' which were prepared by the BMZ. The Accra principles lay down the political guidelines for German development policy in Africa (Mair, 1996, pp. 44–6).

In spite of the difficulty of establishing which of these organisations is predominant, it seems legitimate to suggest that the BMZ has the most important role to play in policy-making on aid to Africa. The BMZ fights for its share of the public budget and it also tries to expand it. In so doing, it forms an alliance with the NGOs and the relatively insignificant part of the public which takes an interest in Africa and development issues. About 20 per cent of the total German aid budget went to sub-Saharan Africa in the first half of the 1990s, and most of it was administered by the BMZ (BMZ, 1996, p. 55).

German NGOs take an active part in influencing official aid policy, including policy towards Africa. However, the NGOs are a very complex group of actors consisting of the party-affiliated political foundations, church-based development organisations and regular non-religious and non-party political development organisations. There is general unanimity that the political foundations are the most important NGOs in German aid and in forming policies towards Africa. Thus, Stefan Mair states:

> The political foundations not only formulate independent interests in the Africa policy of the party to which they are affiliated. They also act as relatively important instruments for German foreign policy because they can exert influence on the internal developments of a given country which is far from what ordinary diplomatic rules allow. (Mair, 1996, p. 51)

There is not much doubt that 'development-policy-oriented NGOs have a substantial impact on German development assistance' (Wiemann,

1997). It has been a deliberate government policy to make use of political foundations, churches, NGOs, and so on to cooperate with and to reach social groups in Africa outside direct government control (Hofmeier, 1994, p. 82). Also, there are several examples of how NGO pressure has forced the government to change its policy in specific fields (Mair, 1996, pp. 54–5).

After the end of apartheid in South Africa, some observers claim that the German NGOs have become more passive. Others argue that the NGOs get more and more influence which might be explained by the lack of serious disagreements between the BMZ and to a large extent also the Ministry of Foreign Affairs and the NGOs. The growing consensus is manifest as the NGOs now openly support the official aid policy of the government.

In general, private industry does not play an important role in German development aid to Africa. In capital aid, as well as in technical cooperation, enterprises increasingly serve as consultants and sub-contractors of the public implementing organisations GTZ and KfW (Nölke and Obser, 1994, p. 23). Because business interests are so limited in Africa, lobbying is of minor importance for aid to the region. The Ministry of Economics even has to work hard to encourage the private sector to engage in the continent by introducing various policy measures to supplement ODA activities (Hofmeier and Schultz, 1984, pp. 229–30). Until now, not much has come out of these initiatives.

On the other hand, business in the form of the agricultural lobby groups is a very influential actor in relation to the BMZ and the Ministry of Economics. The German agricultural lobby is described as 'very strong'. It has had great success fighting against any concessions in trade, especially concerning liberalisation of the imports of agricultural products from any developing country, including the weak African countries. This leaves German policy makers with only the aid card to play while in the mid 1990s concessions on foreign trade seem very unlikely.

Finally, concerning the international determinants of German aid to Africa, Germany finds the close cooperation with the World Bank and the other international aid organisations important. Not least, the World Bank has a special position in German aid policy. Thus, the change from project to programme aid in German development policy was worked out in accordance with the concepts produced by the Bank and the IMF. German support of structural adjustment in Africa was also carried out in close collaboration with the World Bank (Wiemann, 1996).

In spite of the predominant position of the World Bank, there have, in recent years, been attempts to formulate a more independent line in

German development aid thinking *vis-à-vis* the World Bank. But in reality an independent policy has considerable problems because consensus is such an important aim of Germany's external relations. The strong desire for consensus to some extent explains why Germany seldom, if ever, takes strong positions in international fora on development aid or on relations with Africa more generally.

The German policy network

Based on the above, it seems legitimate to describe the German aid policy network as relatively loose as to the contacts between participants. The general lack of conflict within the network can probably be explained by the insignificant material interests in the region which, in turn, permit morality or ethics to play a role as one of the main determinants of German aid to sub-Saharan Africa. That parts of German foreign policy might be influenced by moral values is at least indicated by the speech given by Chancellor Helmut Kohl quoted above.

Due to their official aim, it is to be expected that the BMZ, more or less in agreement with the Ministry of Foreign Affairs and the Ministry of Economics, persistently works in favour of keeping aid to Africa at least at its present level. In that context, there is no doubt the NGOs engaged in Africa are the strongest external supporters of the BMZ. But in recent years, these actors have not been strong enough to prevent cuts in the German aid budget. This is probably due to the lack of any significant popular support for aid and in particular for aid to Africa. The lack of active popular interest in these issues puts the few politicians with an interest in aid, and in Africa, in an extremely weak position when they have to balance the demands for budgets cuts caused by the enormous financial demands for reconstruction of the former GDR.

There are no strong indications that the relationship between the actors described above is very close. On the other hand, this cannot be taken as an indication that the relationship is hostile – rather the contrary. But the loose character of the network may explain why it has been impossible to prevent recent cuts in the budget. The only strong interests in fighting the budget cuts are found within the BMZ and with the NGOs. Both parties have institutional or bureaucratic interests in preventing the cuts as these will potentially threaten their survival.

Having concluded this, there is probably a rock bottom for how much aid to Africa can be cut. As long as the relevant decision makers find that Germany has a moral responsibility towards the poor and less fortunate parts of the world, German aid is not going to disappear totally. But morality might appear to be a very weak determinant if, in the future, it is up against strong material interests demanding cuts.

DENMARK

The official aim of Danish development policy is 'through cooperation with the governments and authorities of the developing countries to support their endeavour to obtain economic growth in order to contribute to securing social progress and political independence in conformity with the Charter of the UN'.

As to the motives of Danish development aid, they have always been a compromise between donor interests and recipient needs, which until the end of the 1980s expressed itself in two opposing development concepts trying to influence the content of bilateral Danish aid. On the one hand, there was the 'trickle down' and, on the other hand, the 'basic needs' approach. In practical politics, the compromise has been reached by guaranteeing the Danish business sector a high return rate without neglecting basic human needs in the actual aid interventions. In recent years, the compromise between trickle down arguments and basic human needs has primarily been secured via the choice of sectors which receive aid in the 20 priority countries of Danish aid, the so-called programme countries.

Health, water and sanitary projects, economic infrastructure plus aid to so-called productive sectors account for a very large percentage of Danish bilateral aid. And these are sectors in which Danish companies have a relative comparative advantage. Prioritising these sectors has not been detrimental to a geographical distribution of bilateral aid. Some 65 per cent of the total has been directed towards low-income countries (Danida, 1995, p. 58). This geographical priority is in line with the overall operational aim of Danish aid which, for more than 20 years, has been specified as 'poverty alleviation'.

The remarkable unanimity among the actors engaged in policy making on aid is primarily to be explained by the existence of strong humanist sentiments which are present in large segments of the Danish population. In political terms, these attitudes find their expression in a widespread support of the ideology of the welfare state, of money being channelled from the more affluent to the less fortunate via the public sector. The welfare state presupposes that people are willing to pay high taxes which until now has been the case. The same attitudes can be identified in development aid where they are designated 'humane internationalism', reflecting a certain consideration for the needs of poor nations which is the main reason why the goal of poverty alleviation has been of such importance in Danish aid.

Traditionally, Denmark has been designated one of the prime representatives of small aid donors which are influenced by humane internationalism. The others are normally considered to be Sweden, Norway, the Netherlands and, to some extent, Canada (Stokke 1989; and Pratt, 1990). It must be emphasised that support for the ideology of poverty alleviation is not in conflict with the views of Danish companies and others that obtain material benefits from being engaged in aid. On the contrary, the general consent to humane internationalism has worked perfectly well with the material benefits which all actors have received from participating in policy making on aid. This goes both for business and for the NGOs which in contrast to other European countries do not depend on charities or on fund-raising activities to any considerable extent.

The ending of the Cold War and the unification of Germany have not had dramatic consequences for Danish foreign-policy priorities; at least these events have not affected relations to Africa. For a number of years, Danish trade with and private investment in Africa have been of minor significance. So, as in the German case, the aid programme is the most important dimension of bilateral relations between Denmark and the programme countries in Africa. Concerning non-programme countries, bilateral relations are, in general, very weak.

Irrespective of this and probably as an expression of the policy priorities of humane internationalism, Denmark has traditionally favoured Africa in its bilateral aid policy. In the 1990s, slightly more than 50 per cent of all bilateral aid has been granted to Africa. The priority given to Africa is a deliberate policy which has been formulated on several occasions and followed by a number of concrete policy initiatives. Thus, the Danish parliament had a debate on Africa in November 1992 which concluded with a resolution to prioritise African development. The same was repeated during the Danish EU Presidency in the spring of 1993.

Actors in Danish aid policy

Since the start of the Danish bilateral aid programme in the 1960s, there have been a number of opinion polls on popular attitudes towards aid. These have shown a steadily growing support for aid. A Gallup poll in February 1995 showed that 75 per cent of the population supported development aid at the current level of 1 per cent of national income (*Berlingske Tidende*, 13 February 1995). Nonetheless, the considerable Danish goodwill towards foreign aid can be questioned. If the populace is asked a more complicated question, namely how their priorities stand as to various expenditures, new surveys indicate that the attitude towards foreign aid is less positive. In 1990, 65 per cent of the Danish population thought that the state spent too much on development aid. These results are in line with the results of the overall European surveys in which respondents are asked to rank policy issues according to their 'importance' (*Eurobarometer*, 44.1, April 1996; and *Eurobarometer* 36, March 1992).

In general, the influence of Danish political parties and the Danish parliament on aid policy towards Africa is limited. This is partly due to the dilemma which the Danish parties face. On the one hand, development aid is in general supported by the electorate (if the opinion polls are to be trusted) while, on the other hand, there are no signs that the votes of the electorate are affected to any appreciable extent by the parties' development policies (Holm, 1982, pp. 110–15; Svendsen, 1989, p. 93).

Therefore, it is relatively cost-free for politicians to have a high personal profile in this policy area and, no doubt, distinct political views can give a high profile without necessarily costing votes because the voters in general take no special interest in the subject. This was illustrated very clearly in 1985 when the Parliament had a major debate on Danish aid policy, initiated by the Social Liberals. As the party seemingly needed to sharpen its own profile while cooperating with the centre-right government on economic policy, it proposed that Danish ODA should be raised to 1 per cent of GDP within a few years.

The government was against the proposal but in the final vote it was defeated. The extraordinary parliamentary consequence of this was that the government accepted defeat – without resigning (Damgaard, 1992, pp. 31–6). This rather confusing situation had to do with the unique parliamentary situation pertaining in Denmark between 1971 and 1993. A significant feature of this period was that all governments were minority governments. This situation gave the political parties quite an extraordinary influence on the policies of the changing governments, including development policy. The small centre parties but also the 'aid constituency' (the interested minority) of the big parties knew how to manipulate these unique parliamentary conditions to promote their own principles and ideas concerning development aid.

Specifically, minority rule gave the numerous small centre parties an opportunity of profound influence since the minority governments depended on the support of these parties in creating coalitions and thereby parliamentary majorities (Damgaard, 1992). This is the basic reason why these parties, and not least the Social Liberals, had substantial influence on the size and to some extent also on the scope of aid policy in those years.

The administrative structure of the Danish aid administration is quite simple compared to the German. Since 1991, there has been a unified foreign service with two administrative groups organised on the basis of geography. One of these, called the 'North group', covers the industrial-ised countries plus the former communist countries in the East, while the other group (called South) covers all the developing countries. The uni-que feature of the 1991 reorganisation of the Danish foreign service is that each of the two groups is responsible for all aspects of Denmark's bilateral relations with a given country, that is, the political, economic, developmental (that is, aid) and – to a certain extent – the commercial (Olsen and Udsholt, 1997).

The broad framework and the lofty principles guiding Danish aid pol-icy, naturally provide extensive latitude to the aid bureaucracy which from the start of Danish bilateral aid in the early 1960s was forced to for-mulate the more concrete policies and the operational guidelines for Danish aid. The only analysis of the influence of the bureaucracy on Danish development aid concludes that 'for many years Danida (that is, the Danish aid administration) has exerted considerable autonomous in-fluence, not only on the concrete adaptation of the aid policy principles but also on the formulation of the policy. Danida's administrative man-agement has in reality decided whether a case or decision is a matter for the executive or for the policy formulating function' (Martinussen, 1989, pp. 245–6). But this autonomy in no way means that Danida is immune to pressure from a wide range of interest groups and private companies.

When Denmark in 1994 acquired a new development aid strategy, it was based on a deliberate 'open door' policy whereby the aid administra-tion invited comments from NGOs, business interests, researchers, and so on during various stages of the preparation of the document. The working process leading up to the final acceptance in parliament of the new aid strategy confirmed once again the dominating role of Danida as the administration itself formulated a whole range of problems to be dis-cussed with the groups and individuals involved. The administration also formulated the policy options, the possible solutions and it presented the ideas about how to implement the new strategy. The whole process, related to the preparation of the 1994 strategy, confirms the conclusion of Martinussen that the aid administration is a very important, if not the most important, determinant of Danish aid.

There are a large number of voluntary organisations engaged in devel-opment issues and in aid-related questions, including both religious and secular organisations. A number of these organisations are heavily engaged in project administration and in the implementation of development projects, often with strong emphasis on popular participation and consciousness-raising among the poor in the developing world. Also, in conformity with their objectives, Danish NGOs undertake general campaigns as well as lobbying Danida in order to influence the content and the implementation of aid policy. Their work is facilitated considerably by the fact that part of their information activities and general operations are financed by the aid administration.

There is no doubt that the NGO community has had considerable leverage on important parts of Denmark's aid policy. The NGOs have contributed to setting the agenda for official Danish policy concerning the necessity of popular involvement in the development process, the special role of women and the importance of the environment. Possibly, the NGOs have been most influential with regard to increasing aid resources. With regard to committing parliament to achieve the 1 per cent target and also, the choice of programme countries for Danish bilateral assistance, both are fields where NGOs have lobbied successfully for focusing attention on Africa and other low-income countries. Thus in a number of instances, the NGOs have first influenced the formulations of broader policy objectives and subsequently held Danida and Parliament accountable.

Since 1991/2, the Danish aid administration has had a special funding scheme for NGOs engaged in development activities. In some cases, official money funds almost 100 per cent of these non-governmental organisations' activities (Danida, 1993). It is argued that the heavy reliance on government funding and the demands for professionalism of project management within NGO administrations lead to a gradual co-optation of these organisations, a tendency which easily can lead to less critical policy positions towards official aid programmes. At least, it can be pointed out that the NGOs are not in general in any kind of strong opposition to the official aid administration, even though from time to time there are disagreements.

At the end of the day, the level of agreement is no doubt greater than the disagreements. When there is 'outside' criticism of Danish aid, the aid administration and the NGO community tend to stand together defending the current features of aid.

In Denmark, the business community is a very important participant in the policy processes related to aid. Their interests are mostly tied to the magnitude of orders and how the individual companies can maximise their earnings from Danish contracts. The informal and often hidden pressure from the business community comes to the surface and is especially evident in relation to choice of sector and programme countries for Danish aid.

In recent years, Danida has launched a number of new initiatives in favour of the private sector. It has established a special Business Secretariat for development assistance designed to promote relations between the business community and aid administration. Also, special programmes have been introduced to support the development of a private sector in developing countries involving active participation from private Danish companies. Finally, the introduction of a mixed-credit scheme intends to make it easier for companies to sell products on the markets in developing countries. All these initiatives illustrate how Danish development policy has taken the interests of the business sector into account without necessarily setting aside other considerations such as poverty alleviation.

Since the mid 1980s, the World Bank has become an increasingly important determinant of Denmark's North–South policy which is narrowly linked to the growing importance of the Bank in relation to the developing countries, and in particular to the poorest countries in Africa which Denmark traditionally has prioritised in its development cooperation. When the World Bank began to move to policy-based lending in the context of structural adjustment programmes in the 1980s and onwards, Denmark initially viewed this with much scepticism.

However, the Danish opposition to structural adjustment reform changed in the mid 1980s and Denmark started to support the position of the World Bank even though this backing was far from uncritical. This policy change was partly provoked by developments in Tanzania, the main recipient of Danish aid since the early 1960s.

The relationship between the Danish aid administration and the World Bank is not only a question of the Bank influencing Danish policies. From 1986 initiatives were taken by the Nordic constituency in the World Bank requesting the Bank to address the social impact of adjustment programmes. However, a thorough assessment of Denmark's specific influence on the World Bank is hampered by the fact that Denmark and the other Nordic countries have not been alone in their criticism.

The Danish aid policy community

The relationship between the actors in Danish aid is both intimate and organised. According to the law guiding Danish development policy, all relevant actors are to be represented on the Board of Danida where they work closely together with the administration. There is also a Council of International Development Cooperation on which all interested organisations and individuals are represented. The members of the Council are free to express their opinion on Danish aid and to criticise whatever they find necessary.

This very orderly network of Danish aid seems to be unique. The more or less daily contacts between the relevant actors tend to merge opposing views over the years. The actors develop common ideas of what are the crucial problems of the sector and accordingly, they tend to develop common attitudes as to which solutions are the most adequate. When a network operates in this way, it is generally called a 'policy community'.

It might very well be that the existence of the aid policy community is the basic explanation as to why Denmark is one of the very few OECD countries not to have cut its aid budget. On the contrary, Denmark has experienced a continuous growth in the total amount of aid allocated to the third world. In this context it should be stressed that all actors in the policy community have got something out of participating, either in terms of influence or material benefits such as jobs, income and profits. That is the case, not only for the business sector, but also Danida and not least the NGOs, who have experienced considerable advantages in curbing disagreements and avoiding the need to politicise aid too much.

No doubt the ideology of poverty alleviation has been very productive in furthering this general agreement. If disagreements were to become too explicit, everybody just has to remind themselves of the overall aim of Danish aid: alleviation of poverty in poor countries. This ideology has also been functional in maintaining the general (though maybe fragile) popular support for the rising aid budget.

The growing aid budget has contributed to giving Denmark a position in international fora not only within development aid. In that respect, the 'big' aid budget measured as per cent of the GNP is functional in furthering overall Danish foreign-policy interests. As Denmark is a small state, it has to use other non-coercive means and instruments to influence developments on the international scene. Aid is one such instrument, and so is the major Danish engagement in UN peace-keeping operations. Both international aid and peace-keeping are in fundamental agreement with Denmark's national interest which is to create international stability, and not least to secure observance to international agreements and rules of conduct.

UK

The official aim of Britain's aid programme is to 'improve the quality of life of people in poorer countries by contributing to sustainable development and reducing poverty and suffering' (HMSO, 1996, pp. 81ff). Within this broad framework, British aid seeks to promote economic growth and reform, promote good government and also to finance activities which directly benefit the poor. As to motives, British aid is a result of a number of cross-cutting interests on political, foreign policy, economic and social affairs. Among the important foreign-policy considerations are the maintenance of Commonwealth links and, in general, the promotion of a stable international environment and thereby stable relations with Britain. Also, the advancement of British trading interests represents an important consideration in aid policy.

Overall, the provision of aid to poor countries is seen as one of the instruments in the Government's wider international policy objective, which stresses the importance of strengthening the UK's commercial and political relations with particular countries. On this basis, it may be reasonable to describe British aid as a 'thoroughly British compromise' (Cassen, 1991, p. 205). In this compromise, altruism may play a role. But when it comes to choosing between altruism and commercial and foreign-policy objectives, Morrissey *et al.* find that 'the developmental and commercial objectives are subsumed within domestic political considerations, and subservient to general political objectives' (Morrissey *et al.*, 1992, p. 2).

Specifying British policy priorities in relation to Africa is rather difficult and, accordingly, it is hard to identify a British policy on Africa. According to Colin Legum, a crucial determinant of British foreign policy is the need for trade and investment (Legum, 1994). Following this logic, the strongest British interest would be to keep good relations with her major trading partners in Africa – Kenya and Nigeria – whereas the rest of sub-Saharan Africa would be of little interest to the British.

This assessment is too simple. At least, it can be argued that Britain's policy towards sub-Saharan Africa is not so unambiguously determined by commercial interests. The UK has a general and long-term interest in the possibility of influencing the course of events in a number of African countries, including Kenya and Nigeria. Not even the end of the Cold War has changed this element of British foreign policy. Therefore, in the 1990s London has a general foreign-policy interest in maintaining a minimum of cordial and close relations to the Commonwealth countries in the continent, irrespective of the relatively insignificant commercial interest of British companies.

These observations seem to be in agreement with Marijke Breuning (1995), who argues that there is a congruence between the rhetoric and the policy behaviour of the decision makers in foreign aid in Britain. The perception of Britain as a 'power broker' is tied very much to the idea that the UK has a special role to play in influencing international developments. The rhetoric of the relevant decision makers seems to support this world view.

Breuning argues that the congruence between the rhetoric and the British aid policy behaviour stems from the power-broker role which manifests itself in a rather low percentage of GNP given as aid plus a high percentage of tied aid (Breuning, 1995). However, the most significant feature of Britain's aid policy might just as well be that it is a part of British foreign policy by emphasising its pro-active stance in creating international coalitions. By building such coalitions supporting British policies, on several occasions London has been in a position to exert influence out of proportion to its weight. This manifests itself in international aid where the UK has been active in establishing the pro-Africa coalition which supports the World Bank's special programme for Africa.

Actors in British aid policy

In Great Britain, neither the public nor the politicians take a strong interest in issues related to third world development. There seems to be a general lack of public interest in overseas aid and third world development. The disappearance of public support for aid is indicated by the younger MPs coming into Parliament. They do not show any particular knowledge of aid and they consider aid an old fashioned issue reflecting 1968 attitudes. A number of observers interpreted this as a consequence of the Conservative governments' successive cuts in development education in schools.

Public opinion surveys on aid have been very infrequent over the years, and they can hardly be characterised as professional – at least it is possible to raise fundamental methodological objections to them. Two privately commissioned surveys of public opinion on aid showed that at the end of the 1980s, the British public in general was in favour of giving aid. But the general scepticism towards opinion polls on aid in Britain does not seem affected by these positive surveys.

One opinion survey concludes that 'the government's performance on overseas aid … simply does not figure among the issues which consistently compete most strongly for the attention of the largest number of voters'

(Burnell, 1991, p. 17). Only very infrequently do third world needs and Britain's involvement in these matters come to the forefront of public concern. And if there is a public awareness of the third world, it is very much related to emergencies and not least emergencies in Africa which shows itself in a passing public readiness to provide charity.

In Britain, Parliament does not play a significant role in aid policy. Full-scale debates on development cooperation seldom take place in the Commons (Burnell, 1991, p. 5). This has very much to do with the fact that aid policy is not generally a matter of legislation. Within Parliament, it is only a small group of MPs which take a strong interest in development matters. The issues and debates in Parliament neither reflect a considerable interest in the electorate nor the interests of an aid constituency for that matter. Therefore, the infrequent debates tend to reflect the interests and concerns of the small group of interested MPs. Because the majority of MPs are not interested in the topic, the relevant ministers tend to pursue their own course (Morrissey *et al.*, 1992, pp. 46–7).

Over the years, Parliament has shown a tendency to become more responsive to outside pressure, especially from pressure groups actively engaged in aid, environment and women (Healey, 1997). This tendency for Parliament to be more actively engaged in aid issues may be correct, in which case Parliament is more or less out of touch with the attitudes of the general public, which is not interested either in development aid or in Africa. Irrespective of whether Parliament tends to be slightly more involved in aid matters than the electorate at large, a preliminary conclusion to the British case is still that Parliament is not very effective on aid policy and therefore, policy making is left largely in the hands of the civil servants of the ODA and maybe with the minister (Bose, 1991, p. 12).

For that reason, lobbying, both from NGOs and commercial interests, depends far more on the relationship to Whitehall and to the government than on the relationship to Parliament. In general, the British aid administration is considered far more influential in policy making than politicians because the ministers do not have the time to involve themselves deeply in all the issues handled in the ODA including expenditure plans, project proposals and, not least, aid implementation. It is characteristic that the implementation of development aid allows great flexibility and thus considerable room for leverage by the bureaucracy. Thus the complexity of aid policy making and the discretion built into the implementation process push the civil servants of the ODA into a pre-eminent position in policy making on aid (Bose, 1991, pp. 128–9; Morrissey *et al.*, 1992, pp. 67, 88).

This dominating position does not exclude the views of the ministers responsible for aid from having a considerable influence on which development issues and objectives are emphasised. According to Morrissey *et al.* 'changes in emphasis that reflect the ideological position of different governments mean that a policy objective will be given greater priority than before and that discretion within a specific area of judgement and decision will be exercised differently' (Morrissey *et al.*, 1992, p. 83).

In line with this, it has to be accepted that the continuously reduced budget for ODA since 1979 is the result of a deliberate policy of Conservative governments. Also, the influence of the minister and the government since 1979 has put very strict limits on any attempts to build empires within the bureaucracy via increasing budgets. So, instead of fighting for larger budget allocations, the game of ODA has for many years been one of resisting decline.

In organisational terms, the ODA is an administrative unit within the Foreign and Commonwealth Office (FCO) with its own minister. It is relatively autonomous in managing aid even though the ODA has to co-ordinate with other departments. *Vis-à-vis* other government departments in Whitehall, the ODA is considered to be a relatively, not to say very, weak agency. There are at least three reasons for this weak position. One is that public spending on overseas aid does not appeal strongly to taxpayers. Secondly it is claimed that public enthusiasm or public support for aid is not widespread in Britain (Burnell, 1991, pp. 15–16). Thirdly, there has never been more than limited support for overseas aid in the Cabinet (Bose, 1991, p. 129).

The three reasons also contribute to explain the continuing decline in British aid and why the cuts have been disproportionate in relation to other public expenditure areas (Morrissey *et al.*, 1992, pp. 162–3). The situation has forced the ODA to rely on external support mainly from the so-called development lobby. This support or the cooperation between the ODA and the development lobby has not been sufficiently effective to prevent the frequent cuts in the aid budget.

In the struggle between different government departments and different external actors, the LDCs – including Africa – have lost out in the battle over the allocation to different regions of the ever-shrinking aid budget. As part of its defensive strategy to keep the aid budget as big as possible, the ODA has turned its attention to Eastern Europe which has been possible because in the British case, aid to Eastern Europe is taken out of the total aid budget. So allocations to sub-Saharan Africa were by the first half of the 1990s down to a little more than 40 per cent of total bilateral allocations. The nadir was 38 per cent for 1995/96 (ODA, 1996, p. 20).

There is general unanimity that the activities of NGOs within Britain's overall development aid are an important trend. Financial assistance from the government to the NGOs has grown rapidly since the beginning of the 1980s, and the dialogue over a number of development issues between government and NGOs has been intensified in the same period (Robinson, 1991, p. 158). This might explain the relative success of the development lobby, including the NGOs, in influencing marginal aspects of British development aid policy such as women in development (WID) and the environment (Morrissey *et al.*, 1992, p. 165).

This relative success of the NGOs does not reflect a corresponding popular support for these organisations. Rather, the development lobby including the NGOs is elitist and technocratic and it works with relatively little connection to the general public. Irrespective of its elitist character, the NGOs represent after all a constituency which is ready to defend NGOs' interests and which in particular is ready to attempt to prevent things from getting worse. It may be helpful to distinguish between the existence of a constituency for narrow NGO interests and a constituency for development in a broader sense. While the first exists and is elitist, it is very hard to identify the latter. Compared to its German and Danish counterparts, the general development lobby is weak. This contributes to explaining why the official aid budget has been reduced ever since 1979 in spite of persistent lobbying by the NGOs.

Furthermore, it has to be stressed that the Conservative governments' large parliamentary majorities (except for the last Conservative victory in 1992) have enabled the government to pursue its own policy priorities without listening to the development lobby. Morrissey argues that the interests of the NGOs and the development lobby cannot easily be represented as economic and political gains for Britain and that, therefore, the Government can 'afford' to overlook the pressure from these groups, which cannot present a uniform view on policy issues apart from very broad ones (Morrissey *et al.*, 1992, p. 64).

However, there are differences between the NGOs. Some have a more direct access to the relevant ministers and to the officials at the ODA, DTI and Treasury. This is the case for Oxfam for example (Morrissey *et al.*, 1992, p. 65). Thus, most observers agree that Oxfam was instrumental in getting the debt relief issue on the agenda of the British position for the G-7 summit meeting in Lyon in 1996. There are also frequent meetings between the ODA and the development NGOs where points of views and information are exchanged. Among the NGOs there seems to be agreement that these meetings do not give influence, rather there is a danger that the voluntary organisations get co-opted by the official system.

In recent years, British NGOs have had to cut their budgets and at the same time they have experienced problems in raising funds from voluntary sources. This has to do with a growing public distrust as to the effectiveness of their project activities, poverty alleviation effects and so on (Edwards and Hulme, 1996, The *Observer*, 20 October 1996). The general distrust is reflected in less willingness to give charity, which is a very different situation from the 'golden days' of the 1980s.

This situation pushes most NGOs into the uncomfortable situation of potentially becoming more and more dependent on the government for funding. This is one of the consequences of the establishment of the 'Joint Funding Scheme', which is a system of joint co-financing administered by the NGOs but financially backed by the government, and which finances 50 per cent of the costs of the NGOs' long-term needs. Mark Robinson claims that 'although it would be an exaggeration to claim that the government has deliberately sought to co-opt NGOs by offering them increased resources, it is nevertheless the case that the voluntary agencies have become more muted in their criticism of the ODA in the 1980s'. The result has been that the relationship with the government has changed from 'one of adversity to one of greater co-operation' (Robinson, 1991, pp. 175–6). However, some NGOs such as Oxfam have a strict policy not to take more than 15 per cent from one source at a time. More funding from a single source would, the organisation thinks, strain its independence.

Robert Cassen claims that the British aid programme is among the most affected by commercial influence (Cassen, 1991, p. 205). There is virtual unanimity in describing British business interests as an important pressure group, comprising major exporting companies organised in such associations as the Confederation of British Industry (CBI) and a number of trade associations and consultants. Business interests have a privileged position in Whitehall where the Department of Trade and Industry (DTI) is the government agency most sympathetic to their demands (Morrissey *et al.*, 1992, p. 57).

British business has had at least two significant types of influence on the character of the UK aid programme. The first shows itself in the high level of procurement tying of bilateral aid. The second is the persistence of the Aid and Trade Provision scheme which is a result of pressure, not least from large firms. On the other hand, it is extremely difficult to evaluate the influence of the CBI, for example, because all dealings between CBI and Whitehall are conducted in confidentiality. However, there seems to be a remarkable convergence of interests between the business lobby, politicians and the civil service which have put business in a position where its interests have gained (Bose, 1991, pp. 136, 143ff).

In recent years, and especially after Margaret Thatcher left office, the ODA has become slightly less closely related to business interests. This has to do with a number of embarrassing cases in which commercial interests have circumvented the aim of official British foreign aid. The scandal of the Pergau Dam in Malaysia speaks for itself. So in some respects, the business community is on the defensive if we compare the 1990s to the 1980s.

The World Bank has had much influence on British foreign aid in a number of areas, even though the relationship has changed since John Major took over in Downing Street. Under Thatcher, Britain tended to follow the directives coming from Washington. According to Paul Mosley, 'the flow of ideas has been from the Bank to the ODA rather than the other way about' (Mosley, 1991, p. 83). Even more strongly, he states that 'the conditionality attached to British programme assistance is simply a photocopy of whatever policy advice has already been offered by the Bank to the sector or authority in question' (*ibid.*, p. 81).

There are several reasons for the prominent position of the World Bank in British foreign aid policy. One is that, over the last three decades, a gradual increase has taken place in the share of the British aid budget which is channelled through multilateral agencies such as the World Bank, the EU and so on. From the point of view of the British government, the World Bank has always been one of the most important development institutions, and the British government has even considered it as a model multilateral institution (Mosley, 1991, p. 83). Keeping close relations with the Washington institutions has been part of the strong British foreign policy priority of having cordial relations with the United States.

In recent years, the relationship between the ODA and the World Bank has been changing. The ODA has become more critical and thus independent in its stance *vis-à-vis* the Bank. British authorities also try to develop alternative concepts for specific development problems and aid issues. Thus, the ODA has hired British researchers to check up on the Bank's operations in sub-Saharan Africa. This has resulted in a number of critical reports which have led to British initiatives within the Bank in order to make the Bank change its policies.

In general, in the 1990s Britain seeks to influence the policies of the Bank to a larger extent than before. In seeking influence, London attempts to build coalitions with like-minded donors in the pursuit of its aims.

The British issue network on aid

The relationship between the actors in the British aid policy network is far less close and far less organised than the Danish case. Contacts between the actors are infrequent and irregular as to who interacts with whom. The British case seems to resemble the 'classical' pressure group situation far more than the other two cases. Thus, business community lobbies put pressure on the relevant government departments. The development lobby also behaves like a classical pressure group; it is worth noting that the regular meetings between the ODA and the NGOs have not developed into anything which can resemble common attitudes and cordial relations – an aid community – which are found especially in the Danish policy community on aid. The British case is far less harmonious than the German or the Danish cases. So, the policy network on aid in Britain is, at most, an issue network, a conclusion which basically is in line with the views held by Morrissey, Smith and Horesh (1992).

Within the network, the ODA has clearly got the upper hand when the focus is narrowly on aid to sub-Saharan Africa. However, due to the special circumstances characterising the British aid budget, the ODA is not necessarily a strong defender of aid to sub-Saharan Africa. The bureaucratic interests of the ODA might be better served by emphasising aid to the former communist countries in eastern Europe instead of defending aid to Africa, which seems to be a 'lost case' with the political circumstances prevailing in the UK.

Thus, the official British aid administration might be a unique example in Europe if it cannot be expected to defend aid to Africa but promotes aid to eastern Europe instead. The strong position of the business community pushes in the same direction, as it has no interest in sub-Saharan Africa. The same is true for the FCO, which traditionally pushes for having relations to as many countries as possible and not least if these countries are important for British business. Remembering that the ODA is a weak department within Whitehall, it is neither surprising that total British official development assistance is shrinking, nor that aid to Africa is under heavy pressure.

Only a strong and active alliance between the NGOs and the ODA might keep Africa on the British agenda. But that does not seem very likely. The NGOs do not have an explicit priority for Africa, and most of them seem to judge that campaign lobbying for Africa in particular is impossible. Put differently, a public campaign for Africa would most probably be a failure, as there is no constituency for that region in Britain.

If Africa is to expect to be on the agenda in the future, it will have to rely on the actual implementation of official British aid by stressing the phrase 'to finance activities which directly benefit the poor'. But for that to happen, such a priority probably has to fit with overall British foreign policy priorities *vis-à-vis* African governments.

Thus, the chances for keeping aid to Africa on the British agenda seem very small as it is difficult to identify actors in the policy network which have an interest in the issue. Compared to the situation in Germany and Denmark, the British case is somewhat discouraging if aid to sub-Saharan Africa is considered to be important for the development of the continent.

DETERMINANTS OF EUROPEAN AID TO AFRICA

A number of observations stand out following the analysis of the policy networks of the three European bilateral donors. First of all, the differences between the three countries are quite considerable and, further, the determinants of aid to sub-Saharan Africa appear to be remarkably weak. A certain element of self-interest is probably a valuable asset, if the relevant actors are expected to struggle hard for aid to Africa. Thus, a minimum of bureaucratic interests rooted both in the official aid administration and in the NGOs probably is the most important determinant. Business interests, public opinion and political/governmental awareness of the topic will no doubt be of minor significance both in the near and the mid-term future.

As to the non-actor determinants of European aid, it cannot be excluded that ethical or moral values combined with a particular role perception of the relevant decision makers might contribute to keep Africa on the European agenda. However, these non-actor determinants must be expected to be rather weak compared to the interests of the actor determinants. The general conclusion to the basic question of this paper is therefore: It is possible to identify determinants which will struggle to keep Africa and aid to the region on the European agenda. But it is doubtful if these determinants are strong enough to maintain aid to sub-Saharan Africa at its current level.

Can this conclusion be applied to the common EU aid, that is, the Lomé aid to Africa? Secondly, can it be generalised to the other 11

European bilateral donors? I would argue that it might very well be, that the conclusion is valid for the Lomé arrangement also. The strength of bureaucratic politics and coalition formation in European politics is not only famous in popular circles, it is also supported by numerous scholarly analyses (Peters, 1992; Bulmer, 1994). There are also solid foundations for claiming that decision-making at the common European level takes place within policy communities which only have a limited number of participants. Thus, it can be argued that if bureaucratic interests are important in policy making on bilateral aid to Africa, they are even more so in the common European policy making on aid.

Are the conclusions presented here valid for the other 11 European bilateral donors? It is probably the case for most countries but not for France, which has strong political/national interests and considerable economic and strategic concerns, particularly in sub-Saharan Africa. Therefore, an analysis of France is definitely inevitable if an adequate answer is to be found to the question of what are the determinants of European aid to sub-Saharan Africa.

References

BMZ (1996) *Zehnter Bericht zur Entwicklungspolitik der Bundersregierung*, Bonn: Bundesministerium für wirtschaftliche Zusammenarbeit und Entwicklung.

Bose, Anuradha (1991) 'Aid and the business lobby', A. Bose and P. Burnell (eds) *Britain's Overseas Aid since 1979: Between Idealism and Self-Interest*, Manchester: Manchester University Press.

Bowles, Paul (1989) 'Recipient Needs and Donor Interests in the Allocation of EEC aid to Developing Countries', *Canadian Journal of Development Studies*, Vol. 10, No. 1, pp. 7–19.

Breuning, Marijke (1995) 'Words and Deeds: Foreign Assistance Rhetoric and Policy Behaviour in the Netherlands, Belgium and the United Kingdom', *International Studies Quarterly*, Vol. 39, pp. 235–54.

Bulmer, Simon J. (1994) 'The Governance of the European Union: A New Institutionalist Approach', *Journal of Public Policy*, Vol. 13, No. 4, pp. 351–80.

Burnell, P. (1991) 'Introduction to British Overseas Aid: Between Idealism and Self-Interest', A. Bose and P. Burnell (eds) *Britain's Overseas Aid since 1979: Between Idealism and Self-Interest*. Manchester: Manchester University Press, pp. 1–31.

Carlsnaes, Walter (1992) 'The Agency-Structure Problem in Foreign Policy Analysis', *International Studies Quarterly*, Vol. 36, No. 3, pp. 245–70.

Cassen, Robert (1991) 'Afterword', A. Bose and P. Burnell (eds) *Britain's Overseas Aid since 1979: Between Idealism and Self-Interest*, Manchester: Manchester University Press.

Damgaard, Erik (1992) 'Denmark: Experiments in parliamentary government', E. Damgaard (ed.) *Parliamentary Change in the Nordic Countries*, Oslo: Scandinavian University Press.

Danida (1993) *Strategi for Danidas NGO-samarbejde. Situations – og perspektivanalyse*, Copenhagen: Danida.

Danida (1995) *Danidas aarsberetning 1995*, Copenhagen: Danida.

Edwards, Michael and D. Hulme (1996) 'Too Close for Comfort? The Impact of Official Aid on Nongovernmental Organizations', *World Development*, Vol. 24, No. 6, pp. 961–73.

Ghils, Paul (1992) 'International civil society: International non-governmental organizations in the international system', *International Social Science Journal*, Vol. 133, pp. 417–32.

Healey, John (1997) 'UK Aid Management', C. Cox, J. Healey, A. Koning (eds) *How European Aid Works: A Comparison of Management Systems and Effectiveness*, London: Overseas Development Institute.

Hill, Christopher (1996) 'United Kingdom: sharpening contradictions', C. Hill (ed.) *The Actors in European Foreign Policy*, London: Routledge, pp. 68–89.

HMSO (1996) Foreign and Commonwealth Office including Overseas Development Administration, *1996 Department Report: The Government's Expenditure Plans 1996–7 to 1998–9*, London.

Hofmeier, Rolf (1994) 'German–African Relations: Present and Future', S. Brüne, J. Betz, W. Kühne (eds), *Africa and Europe: Relations of Two Continents in Transition*, Hamburg: LIT Verlag, pp. 71–86.

Hofmeier, Rolf and S. Schultz (1984) 'German aid: Policy and Performance', Olav Stokke (ed.) *European Development Assistance. Policies and Performance*, Vol. 1, Oslo: Norwegian Institute of International Affairs.

Holm, H.-H. (1982) *Hvad Denmark gor... En analyse of dansk u-landspolitik*, Aarhus: Politica.

Hook, Steven W. (1995) *National Interest and Foreign Aid*. Boulder: Lynne Rienner.

Kegley, Ch. W. (1992) 'The New Global Order: The Power of Principle in a Pluralistic World', *Ethics and International Affairs*, Vol. 6.

Legum, Colin (1994) 'Britain's Policy in Africa', S. Brüne *et al.*, *Africa and Europe: Relations of Two Continents in Transition*, Hamburg: LIT Verlag.

Lipschutz, R.D. (1992) 'Reconstructing World Politics. The Emergence of Global Civil Society', *Millennium: Journal of International Studies*, Vol. 21, No. 3, pp. 389–420.

Mair, Stefan (1996) *Deutsche Interessen in Afrika Südlich der Sahara*, Stiftung Wissenschaft und Politik, Ebenhausen, SWPIP 2961, Juni.

Maizels, Alfred and M.K. Nissanke (1984) 'Motivations for Aid to Developing Countries', *World Development*, Vol. 12, No. 9, pp. 879–900.

March, J. and J. Olsen (1989) *Rediscovering Institutions*, New York: Free Press.

Martin, Guy (1995) 'Continuity and Change in Franco-African Relations', *Journal of Modern African Studies*, Vol. 33, No. 1, pp. 1–20.

Martinussen, John (1989) 'Danidas handlingsplan. Et essay on administrationens rolle i formuleringen af dansk bistandspolitik', B. Heurlin and C. Thune (eds) *Danmark og det internationale system*, Copenhagen: Politiske studier.

McGillivray, Mark, and Howard White (1993) *Explanatory Studies of Aid Allocation among Developing Countries: A Critical Survey*, Working Paper Series No. 148. The Hague: Institute of Social Studies.

Morrissey, Oliver, Brian Smith, and Edward Horesh (1992) *British Aid and International Trade*. Buckingham: Open University Press.

Mosley, Paul (1991) 'Britain, the World Bank and Structural Adjustment', A. Bose & P. Burnell (eds) *Britain's Overseas Aid since 1979: Between Idealism and Self-Interest*. Manchester: Manchester University Press, pp. 74–85.

Noël, Alain, and Jean-Philippe Thérien (1995) 'From domestic to international justice: the welfare state and foreign aid', *International Organization*, Vol. 49, No. 3, pp. 523–53.

Nölke, Andreas and A. Obser (1994) 'Coordinating the Development Policies of European Countries – Case Study of the Development Aid Policies of Germany', Rhi-Sausi, J.L. and M. Dassu (eds) *Coordinating Aid Policies of European Countries*, Vol. 1, National Case Studies, Rome: Centro Studi Political Internationale.

ODA (1996) *British Aid Statistics 1991/92–1995/96*, East Kilbride: Overseas Development Administration.

OECD (1997) *Development Co-operation. 1996 Report*. Paris: OECD.

Olsen, G. Rye and L. Udsholt (1997) 'Danish Aid Management', Aidan Cox *et al.*, *How European Aid Works: A Comparison of Management Systems and Effectiveness* London: Overseas Development Institute.

Peters, Guy (1992) 'Bureaucratic Politics and the Institutions of the European Community', Alberta M. Sbrabia (ed.) *Euro-Politics. Institutions and Policy-making in the 'New' European Community*. Washington: The Brookings Institution, pp. 75–122.

Petersen, Nikolaj (1995) 'Denmark's Foreign Policy since 1967: An Introduction', G. Due-Nielsen and N. Petersen (eds) *Adaptation and Activism. The Foreign Policy of Denmark 1967–1993*, Copenhagen: DJOEF Publishing, pp. 11–54.

Pratt, Cranford (1990) (ed.) *Middle Power Internationalism. The North–South Dimension*, Kingston, Ontario: McGill-Queen's University Press.

Rhodes, R.A.W. and D. Marsh (1992) 'New Directions in the Study of Policy Networks', *European Journal of Political Research*, Vol. 21, No. 1–2, pp. 191–205.

Robinson, Mark (1991) 'An uncertain partnership: the Overseas Development Administration and the voluntary sector in the 1980s', A. Bose and P. Burnell (eds) *Britain's Overseas Aid since 1979: Between Idealism and Self-Interest*, Manchester: Manchester University Press.

Rosenau, J.N. (1992) 'Normative Challenges in a Turbulent World', *Ethics and International Affairs*, Vol. 6.

Rummel, Reinhardt (1996) 'Germany's role in the CFSP: Normalität or Sonderweg?', C. Hill (ed.) *The Actors in European Foreign Policy*, London: Routledge, pp. 40–67.

Schraeder, Peter J. (1995) 'From Berlin 1984 to 1989: Foreign Assistance and French, American, and Japanese Competition in Francophone Africa', *Journal of Modern African Studies*, Vol. 33, No. 4, pp. 539–67.

Shaw, Martin (1992) 'Global Society and Global Responsibility: The Theoretical, Historical and Political Limits and International Society', *Millennium: Journal of International Studies*, Vol. 21, No. 3, pp. 421–34.

Smith, Martin J. (1993) *Pressure Power & Policy. State Autonomy and Policy Networks in Britain and the United States*, Hempel Hempstead: Harvester-Wheatsheaf.

Stokke, Olav (ed.) (1989) *Western Middle Powers and Global Poverty. The Determinants of the Aid Policies of Canada, Denmark, the Netherlands, Norway and Sweden*. Uppsala: Scandinavian Institute of African Studies.

Svendsen, Knud Erik (1989) 'Danish Aid: Old Bottles', O. Stokke (ed.), *Western Middle Powers and Global Poverty*, Uppsala: Scandinavian Institute of African Studies.

Wiemann, Jürgen (1997) 'German Development Aid', Aidan Cox *et al.*, *How European Aid Works: A Comparison of Management Systems and Effectiveness*, London: Overseas Development Institute.

8 Does European Aid Work? An Ethiopian Case Study[*]

Simon Maxwell

INTRODUCTION

The European Union is never short on controversy; and in the sphere of development aid, a business now worth $US 5 billion a year to the EU,[1] there is certainly much to discuss at present. In 1995, the mid-term review of Lomé IV was completed and an acrimonious dispute was settled about the level of funding available to the year 2000: in neither case was the outcome particularly favourable to developing countries.[2] Beginning in 1996, attention has turned to the future of development aid after that time, when Lomé IV expires. Here, a Green Paper has been published by the Commission (EC 1996) and there is a many-layered debate. Negotiations will begin in the second half of 1998. The debate ranges from the high politics of first world–third world relations within the grand European project, itself the subject of the on-going Inter-Governmental Conference, to internal issues such as how to allocate development portfolios within the Directorates General of the European Commission.

As the debate evolves, in think tanks, conferences and position papers,[3] it is possible to discern two alternative visions of the future of European development aid, no doubt with gradations in between. As visions go, these maximalist and minimalist versions of the future do not come entirely out of the blue.[4] They do, however, have brand new features, reflecting contemporary events like the debate on subsidiarity, the Final Act of the GATT, the apparent tilt of EU priorities towards the Mediterranean, and the prospective enlargement of the EU to embrace countries in Eastern Europe. Table 8.1 provides a schematic outline of the two competing visions, and in so doing helps to map the current debate about the future of European development aid.

---

* Paper presented to a conference, 'Europe and the Developing Countries', organised by the European Development Policy Study Group of the Development Studies Association of UK and Ireland, and held on 17 October 1996 at the Offices of the European Parliament in London. Helpful comments on an earlier draft were received from Chris Stevens and Sean Doyle. Responsibility, of course, is mine.

At one extreme, the maximalist position aspires to the continuation of a contractual aid and trade partnership with the 71 countries of the ACP Group, running in parallel and perhaps linked to programmes for other regional groupings, like Asia and the Mediterranean. The vision is of an aid programme enlarged and strengthened, so that aid channelled through the European Commission, so-called 'community action', comes to assume a large share of total aid from European countries to the developing world: bilateral aid, or 'national action' might, on this vision, eventually wither away. Growth would be accompanied by the development of greater policy expertise, so that the Commission would finally emerge as a heavyweight player in policy dialogue, acting as a counter-balance to the 'Washington consensus' of the Bretton Woods Institutions. The maximalist would require administrative reorganisation, and greater political accountability through the European Parliament. In principle, this is certainly an attractive vision.

Table 8.1   Maximalist and minimalist positions for the evolution of European aid

	Maximalist position	Minimalist position
Geographical coverage	Priority to 71 ACP countries, parallel to programmes for other regional blocs	All developing countries indiscriminately
Substantive coverage	Aid and trade	Aid only
Contractuality and partnership	Yes – renew Lomé	No – abandon Lomé
Finance	Maintain non-budgetary European Development Fund	Budgetize all aid
Size of programme	Increasing – maximise Commission 'acquis'	Decreasing – 'renationalize' wherever possible
Scope of programme	Broad – cover all aid instruments, engage in policy dialogue with recipient countries	Narrow – specialize in sector and project aid, leave policy dialogue to Bretton Woods Institutions and humanitarian aid to the UN
Political accountability	More control by European Parliament	Maintain control by Member States through Development Council
Administration	Create European Development Agency	Simplify and streamline existing bureaucracy

The minimalist position, by contrast, seeks to fetter the growth of EU aid and to 'renationalise' wherever possible, so that member-state programmes predominate. It sees little value in preserving the contractual nature of the Lomé agreement, especially since trade preferences have been eroded by the GATT; and it points to the inconsistency that many poor countries, especially those in South Asia, are not members of the ACP. On this reading, the minimalists would prefer a unified aid budget, covering all traditional countries, and run along traditional lines by a smaller and less dispersed aid administration in Brussels. They would maintain political control of the programme through the Development Council and its network of committees, rather than through the Parliament.

Adjudicating between these competing visions of the future – or negotiating a compromise between them – is partly a matter of political preference. However, policy analysis can also play a part, by illuminating the costs and benefits of different routes. Here, the key issue is quality. Is European aid in some sense 'better' than, or equivalent to, bilateral aid provided by member states – or, indeed, through the World Bank and the UN? If the answer to this question is positive, then there may be unequivocal benefits in moving towards the maximalist position. If, on the other hand, the answer is negative, then movement will be determined by whether the cost represented by lower quality is justified by political or other benefits.

Now, the question about aid quality is difficult to answer. It is difficult enough to establish whether or not aid has positive effects on growth, poverty reduction and social welfare, even in the aggregate, for all countries and all donors (White, 1992; Mosley and Hudson, 1995). It is much more difficult to do so for individual donors and individual countries (White, 1995; Mosley and Hudson, 1995). The problem is made more complex when what is asked for is a comparison between one form of aid (community action) and another (national action). Despite the breadth and historical depth of the literature on aid, this is a question that is only beginning to be asked.[5]

In principle, there should of course be great advantages in European aid, as a slightly special form of multilateral aid. Comparing community action with national action (though not with UN or other 'pure' multilateral aid) there should be economies of scale, greater cost-effectiveness in procurement, clearer lines of political accountability, and simplification of administration. The EU also has a role, enshrined in the Maastricht Treaty, in the coordination of all aid from member states.

The study which this paper summarizes does not provide answers to the comparative questions. However, as the first full-scale evaluation of European aid to a single country, it does shed light on the question 'Does European Aid Work?'; and in so doing, begins to illuminate the political debate between maximalists and minimalists.

We need to advance in stages. The next section offers a brief exploration of what might be meant by the idea of aid 'working' or 'not working'. The third section summarises the findings of the Ethiopia study, and the section following from that explores the implications for the debate on European aid. In brief, the paper concludes that some EU aid to Ethiopia, perhaps most, 'worked', but some did not – for reasons partly internal to Ethiopia and partly internal to the EU. The EU programme has improved markedly but could improve further: a seven-point action programme is proposed to enable the EU to achieve an objective-driven strategy. A shift of resources from national action to community action would then be justified, capitalising on the economies of scale and the scope for more effective policy dialogue. A European Development Agency would also become an attractive idea.

MEASURING AID PERFORMANCE

Writing originally in 1985, Cassen and Associates (1994, p. 6) defined aid effectiveness in development terms, deliberately excluding political and commercial considerations:

> Does aid contribute macro-economically or otherwise to growth? Does it reach the poor? ... Does aid help or hinder an appropriate functioning of market forces?

These questions have received much attention in the research-based academic literature (White, 1995; Mosley and Hudson, 1995). The results are mixed. Acknowledging the difficulties of evaluation, Cassen and Associates (1994, p. 7) reached 'at least a well-educated assessment' that 'most aid works'. Similarly, Mosley and Hudson (1995, p. 11), quoting World Bank data, describe the 'positive direct effect of projects, as evidenced by the overwhelming positive rates of return reported at ex-post evaluation'. At the aggregate level, however, the indicators are less encouraging: summarising a variety of studies, Mosley and Hudson (1995, p. 11) conclude that 'the average impact of overseas aid [is] low or even neutral'. In the case of British aid to a sample of countries, 'significant influence on...under 5 mortality is achieved more frequently than significant influence on growth' (*ibid.*, p. 6).

In the evaluation literature, mostly sponsored by aid agencies, aid performance has been approached more on a project-by-project basis, though sometimes at the sector level or by instrument (for example, food aid). At the same time, there has been less attention to overall impact in terms of the criteria set out by Cassen, and more to other aspects of performance. The inspiration here has been the logical framework, which sets out a structure for the relationship between inputs and overall development objectives, and also defines different levels of evaluation. These are reproduced in Figure 8.1, which distinguishes between efficiency, effectiveness and impact evaluation. The first is concerned with the outputs of a project (for example 'extension services provided'), the second with short-term objectives or purposes (for example 'increase crop yields or agricultural output') and only the third with poverty reduction or growth (for example 'increase income or reduce poverty'). Thus, the term 'effectiveness', as used by Cassen, is here redefined as impact.

In practice, many evaluation studies do not consider impact, regarding the long-term outcomes of projects as being somewhat remote from the inputs provided by aid, and subject to the influence of many external factors beyond the control of the project. Thus the EU, for example, tends to concentrate on relevance, efficiency and effectiveness, defining them as in the box below.

Relevance, effectiveness and efficiency

Relevance: assesses the problems to be solved and the project objectives against their physical and policy 'environment', for example, the main features of the sector and pertinent policies of the various actors.

Effectiveness: assesses the extent to which the project results have contributed towards the achievement of the project purpose or whether this can be expected to happen in the future on the basis of the current results of the project.

Efficiency: assesses whether the activities have been carried out efficiently in order to yield the project results. Have the means of the project been efficiently transformed through the project's activities into the various project results? Could the same or similar results have been achieved at lower cost?

Source: 'Evaluation Report Lay-out', EU Commission, Feb. 1995.

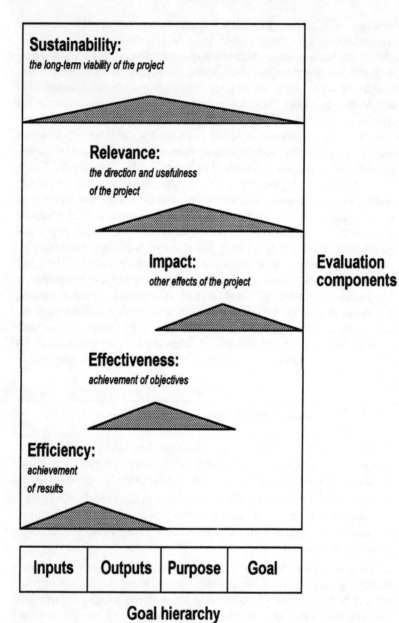

Sustainability:
the long-term viability of the project

Relevance:
the direction and usefulness
of the project

Impact:
other effects of the project

**Evaluation
components**

Effectiveness:
achievement of objectives

Efficiency:
achievement
of results

| Inputs | Outputs | Purpose | Goal |

Goal hierarchy

Figure 8.1   An evaluation model for analysing development assistance projects
Source: Norway, 1993, p. 23.

Three problems remain, even with the limits on evaluation set out in Box 1. First, 'aid' consists of many heterogeneous activities, some of which are much more difficult to evaluate than others. Standard evaluation methodology is derived from project-level social cost-benefit analysis, in which direct effects can be identified and measured. This is not so easy in the case of programme aid (White and Toye (eds), 1996), technical cooperation (Berg, 1993; Fukuda-Parr, 1995) or other forms of aid which may have economy-wide benefits or substantial non-monetary benefits. Limiting evaluation to effectiveness and not impact simplifies the problem but does not entirely remove it.

The second problem is that of comparators. Against what standard is aid performance to be measured? Again, this is a relatively straightforward problem in cost-benefit analysis, where standard minimum rates of return can be defined, but is more difficult for non-project aid, and when it comes to defining effectiveness and efficiency. It is necessary for any evaluation to define its benchmarks in advance.

Finally, the task of evaluation is not just to measure performance, but also to explain it. Explaining means addressing a new set of issues, which can be described as 'systemic': these refer to the attributes of the donor or the recipient, and are the areas in which recommendations need to be made (Maxwell, 1997).

EUROPEAN AID TO ETHIOPIA, 1976–94

Introduction

As noted above, the Ethiopia evaluation was the first full-scale study of European aid to a single country. Field work was carried out in March 1995, and a seven-volume report was published in June 1996 (IDS and IDR, 1996). The task of the evaluation was to assess the relevance, effectiveness and efficiency of European aid. In addition, it was concerned with the management of the programme as a whole, both by the EU and by the Government of Ethiopia, and with the policies, procedures and administration of the EU aid system.

The methodological problems were those outlined in the previous section, namely the heterogeneity of the programme, the question of comparators and the need to identify underlying systemic issues. The methods used to overcome these problems included documentary analysis, key informant interviews, site visits, a limited amount of participatory rural appraisal, and five focus group discussions. The team also made use of the logical framework and of a specially designed evaluation scoring system (IDS and IDR, 1996, pp. 2ff).

In terms of comparators, the team made reference to DAC best-practice guidelines (OECD, 1992) and to the EU's own policy documents (IDS and IDR, 1996, pp. 117ff). The focus group discussions provided both a checklist of systemic issues and initial bench-marking of the EU against other donors (Maxwell, 1997). The checklist is reproduced in Table 8.2 and provides a kind of best-practice charter for donors and recipients.

Table 8.2   Best practice criteria: a synthesis of focus group discussions

How to be a good donor	How to be a good recipient	How to be a good NGO
1. A clear development philosophy	1. Respect for human rights and liberty of press	1. Clear objectives
2. A wide range of instruments	2. Internal peace and stability	2. Communication and coordination with Government
3. A high grant element	3. A commitment to development	3. Capacity-building and use of local structures
4. Low tying of aid	4. Clear long- and medium-term strategies	4. Flexibility
5. A jointly negotiated aid framework	5. A commitment to open and constructive policy dialogue at macro and sector levels	5. Community participation
6. A capacity for policy analysis	6. A good working relationship with donors	6. Advocacy
7. Constructive policy dialogue	7. The technical and administrative capacity to identify, prepare and appraise projects for donor financing	7. Attention to women's issues
8. A long-term commitment	8. Clear lines of authority for decentralised planning and project implementation	8. Accountability – to the people, government and donors
9. A capacity for sector analysis and planning	9. A commitment to beneficiary participation	9. Transparency

10. Cooperation with other donors

11. A commitment to genuine recipient and stake-holder participation in project selection and design

12. Systematic and transparent project appraisal and approval procedures

13. Decentralised decision-making and management

14. High technical capacity in field offices and headquarters

15. Continuity of project management

16. Flexibility on the ground in project operations

17. Quick, simple, open procedures for financing and procurement

18. Effective monitoring and evaluation, leading to change

19. A high level of accountability

10. A commitment to meeting staffing and local cost provisions for projects

11. The absence of corruption

12. Good administration and accounting

13. Timely monitoring and reporting

14. A commitment to self-criticism and learning

10. Low overheads and good administration

11. Compliance with government guidelines

12. Ability to link relief with development by adopting an integrated approach

13. Coordination between NGOs

14. Use of local resources and structures

15. Support to local NGOs

16. Few expatriate staff and employment opportunities for nationals

17. Effective and efficient use of resources

18. Quality and timeliness of reporting

Source: IDS and IDR, 1996, Appendix VII.

'Hitting a moving target from a moving platform'

The EU committed over 2 billion ECU in 1990 prices in aid to Ethiopia between 1976 and 1994, equivalent to about $ US 2.5 billion. The programme included both emergency relief and development aid. It drew on a wide variety of aid instruments available from the EU. And it touched almost every sector of the Ethiopian economy. Figure 8.2

illustrates the evolution of the programme over the period. It shows both substantial growth and a changing distribution. At the beginning of the period, in the Lomé I phase, most commitments fell under the National Indicative Programme (NIP), the main vehicle for disbursement under the European Development Fund. By Lomé III, the situation had changed as food aid (financed from the budget) became an important feature of aid to Ethiopia, and as Stabex also grew in importance. In Lomé IV, food aid remained substantial, Stabex grew even larger, and further diversification was brought about by the introduction of a new window for Structural Adjustment Support (SAS).

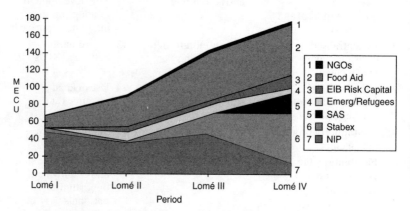

Figure 8.2   Aid flow to Ethiopia, 1976–1993: average annual commitments by Lomé Agreement (at constant 1990 ECU)
NB: Lomé IV excludes Eritrea
Source: IDS and IDR, 1996.

These changes illustrate the evolution of the EU aid programme over the period, particularly the diversification of instruments in Lomés III and IV.[6] There were other changes too, particularly the increasing level of policy dialogue and policy conditionality in Lomés III and IV. Whereas the Lomé I and II periods were dominated by the idea of contractuality, in which the recipient countries took the lead in defining aid programmes, Lomés III and IV saw the gradual erosion of this principle, and its replacement with a more conventional approach. This tendency has been further reinforced in the mid term review of Lomé IV.

At the same time, Ethiopia itself underwent major changes during the evaluation period. For most of that time, a socialist regime led by Mengistu Haile Mariam ruled the country, though engaged in a constantly escalating civil war which finally led to the overthrow of the regime in 1991 and the secession of Eritrea in 1993. The regime followed Stalinist policies until the late 1980s, characterised by pervasive state control of the economy, forced villagisation of the peasantry and compulsory resettlement programmes. In 1988, there was a partial liberalisation, followed in 1990 by a comprehensive move to a market economy. This process continued under the new government.

Changes of this magnitude on both the donor and recipient sides muddy the waters of evaluation. More importantly, they greatly complicated the planning and management of the aid relationship. The National Indicative Programme for Lomé IV, for example, due just at the time the Mengistu regime was overthrown, had effectively to be negotiated three times – and continuing negotiations with the new Government meant that four years into the Lomé period, at the end of 1994, only 20 per cent of the resources earmarked had been committed. In any case, it is important not to judge the programme by standards that were inappropriate at the time, and to take into account the problem of 'hitting a moving target from a moving platform'.

Sectoral perspectives

Figure 8.3 illustrates the sectoral distribution of EU aid expenditure over the evaluation period. On the development side, infrastructure was the dominant sector in Lomés I and II, agriculture took over in Lomé III, and programme aid (including Stabex) has been dominant in Lomé IV. These sectoral priorities reflected changing thinking in successive Lomé agreements. Food aid grew rapidly, as can be seen, and was mostly destined for emergency purposes, although a proportion was used for development projects and, latterly, for sale to support the market and generate counterpart funds.

Within these broad parameters, the EU supported a wide variety of activities: large agricultural projects, like the Shoa Peasant Area Development Project (PADEP) and the Coffee Improvement Programme; major infrastructure, like water supply for Addis Ababa or the power line for Dessie; hospitals and roads, fertiliser imports and budget support, NGO co-financing projects; and, of course, a very large volume of food aid.

The evaluation 'story' told by this heterogeneous package is inevitably complex. The activities cover different kinds of aid, trying to achieve different things, in different places, and at different moments in the evolution of European aid policy and Ethiopian political economy. Much good work was accomplished, and very many lives were saved by emergency relief.

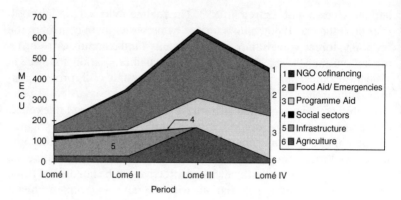

Figure 8.3   EU aid commitments to Ethiopia by evaluation sector, 1976–93 (in constant 1990 ECU)
NB: Lomé IV excludes Eritrea

A number of themes run through the evaluation reports: the enormous difficulties of 'doing business' in Mengistu's Ethiopia; the negative impact of an unfavourable policy environment; the challenges posed by repeated shocks, whether climatic, political or economic; 'learning by doing' and gradual improvement in the quality of the EU programme; but nevertheless a mixed record of success and failure, with scope for further improvement.

In general, it was evident that some activities out-performed others. Thus, in infrastructure, water and energy, the large engineering projects, like the Amarti Diversion project or the Addis Ababa water supply project, were more successful than the geographically scattered and socially complex projects, like rural water supply. In the agriculture field, also, the technology-driven projects, like Amibara irrigation and Central Shoa PADEP, seemed to out-perform projects in more difficult physical and social environments, like soil conservation projects. In the programme aid sector, the agricultural Sectoral Import Programme, another fairly straightforward project, scored more highly than more complex alternatives, notably Stabex.

It was difficult to reach generalisations about comparative sectoral performance. However, it was notable that the food aid and agriculture/ rural development evaluations were generally less favourable than those of the other sectors.

These findings, it has to be said, are not unfamiliar in the aid evaluation literature: a mixed pattern of success and failure, the difficulty of managing socially-complex poverty reduction projects, the dominant importance of the recipient country's domestic policy environment – all these are themes common to most analyses of aid (see, for example, Cassen and Associates, 1994). The interesting evaluation question is how far the pattern of success and failure can be explained by the attributes of the donor agency and by the quality of the aid relationship it enjoyed. It is in examining this question that we come closer to the underlying quality questions about European aid.

Thematic issues[7]

The analysis of thematic issues in the evaluation report is carried out under the headings of 'relevance', 'effectiveness' and 'efficiency'. The following is a brief and partial summary.

Relevance: policy, planning and programming

In terms of overall relevance, the EU aid programme in Ethiopia certainly addressed issues of fundamental importance to one of the poorest countries of the world. There can be no criticism of the programme for concentrating on rural infrastructure and rural development, for providing a large amount of food aid, especially during and after the great famine of 1984/85, or for supporting economic liberalisation and structural adjustment through the Emergency Recovery and Reconstruction Programme after 1991. The large infrastructure projects in energy and water supply also appear to have met a genuine need.

The issues that arise are more subtle: first, the political question of providing aid to a totalitarian regime in the 1970s and 1980s; secondly, questions about critical mass and integration of instruments; and, thirdly, an issue about the capacity to engage in the policy analysis and policy dialogue required to mount successful projects.

The political issue was not trivial for a country with a very poor human rights record and the status of a pariah state among most other Western donors. EU development aid unfortunately provided some moral comfort to the regime and may have supported the war indirectly. Under Lomés I and II, the EU formally had no room for manoeuvre and was bound by the contractuality provisions of the Convention.[8] Under Lomé III, when conditions changed, the EU engaged in a major programme of policy dialogue. It is ironic that the EU finally 'geared up' to handle difficult regimes, just at the time when Ethiopia was moving rapidly in the EU's direction.

On critical mass and integration of instruments, by far the biggest problem was the lack of linkage between food aid and other instruments, caused by different sources of funding and different planning procedures. As a result, food and financial aid were largely directed to different parts of the country and opportunities for complementarity, including in policy dialogue, were missed. There were similar problems with other budget lines (of which there are more than 30 altogether, though not all applicable to Ethiopia).

The multiplicity of aid instruments and the complexity of the EU programme in Ethiopia suggest that a single country programme is needed. Yet the planning cycle for the five-yearly National Indicative Programmes has not met the need, because a large part of aid has been outside the NIP. A more general country strategy has, however, been prepared for the Lomé IV *bis* period, covering 1996–2000.

As country programmes are prepared, and as these are then turned into sectoral programmes and finally into projects, a capacity to carry out policy dialogue is essential. The EU was weak on policy dialogue until Lomé III, for reasons already discussed. It took important initiatives under Lomé III and made a positive contribution, along with other donors and reformers within the Government. There were other success stories later, for example the leadership role of the EU in negotiating a new approach to the management of counterpart funds. Nevertheless, performance on policy dialogue was uneven. The EU was repeatedly described to the evaluation team as 'punching below its weight'.

Effectiveness and sustainability

On effectiveness and sustainability, the main issue which arose was the unfavourable policy environment during much of the period reviewed. However, there were also some problems with project design, and with the lack of continuity of support to some projects.

Many projects would have seemed much more successful in retrospect had the policy environment been better. The policy of the Mengistu Government had some positive features, including the land reform of 1975 and the commitment to literacy campaigns in the late 1970s and early 1980s. However, the overall balance was negative: in terms of market control and pricing, problems of state-sponsored institutions, and poor policy, including forced villagisation and resettlement. The war also had an important negative effect: apart from the loss of life and the cost, a great deal of infrastructure was damaged or destroyed. Several

EU-supported institutions were looted during the final days of the Mengistu regime.

In terms of project design, there was a general problem with over-centralisation and over-standardisation, reflecting a bias of the Ethiopian Government that the EU should perhaps have done more to challenge. More generally, EU projects would have benefited from the preparation of stronger appraisal reports, and from earlier adoption of the logical framework as a planning tool. The standards of project cycle management appeared to be higher for EDF-funded projects than for projects funded by EU budget lines.

Support to particular projects was sometimes insufficient. The discontinuities between Lomés may help to account for this. At the same time, field-level initiatives were hampered by long chains of decision-making back to Brussels.

Efficiency: management, supervision and reporting

Questions of management, supervision and reporting featured prominently in key informant interviews and focus group discussions. In the focus groups, for example, speed of decision-making, efficiency of administration and project management were all cited as areas where the EU compared unfavourably with other donors. In many cases, routine project management was favourably evaluated, presumably as a result of the joint effort of Ethiopian Government staff and EU contractors. However, problems were cited on the Government side, and also, very forcefully, on the side of the EU. The main problem areas were delegation of authority, staffing, procedures, and reporting.

The issue of decentralisation is best exemplified by the lack of delegated authority to approve projects at the country level, a situation which contrasts markedly with other donors. It has costs in terms of the long delays in the system: up to a year to approve an NGO project or a Framework of Mutual Obligations for Stabex, and long delays in procurement. The problem is compounded by overly complex procedures. It seemed that the word 'Delegation' was a misnomer for EU field offices.

The problem of under-staffing was manifest in the lack of junior professional and support staff to assist Delegation Advisers and the desk officer in Brussels. USAID, for example, had 25 local professional staff in Addis Ababa (excluding administration and public relations), the EU had none. This was particularly surprising, as one EU international staff member cost at least twenty times as much as a similarly well-qualified Ethiopian recruited locally.

Food aid provided an extreme case of lack of professional input at the field level. In 1994, there was one logistics specialist, with little policy role or local administrative support, to monitor a programme costing over 30 per cent of total EU commitments to Ethiopia. Partly as a result, the Delegate and other officials, with other responsibilities, were drawn into the food aid programme. A new unit had, however, just been established in the Delegation, adding two additional posts.

The staffing problem had a number of knock-on costs. One was the heavy reliance on consultants, which had adverse consequences for continuity. For example, the Coffee Improvement Project had been subject to at least six different reviews, each undertaken by a different consultant organisation.

Finally, on monitoring and evaluation, the sectoral reports identified a need for more evaluation of project effects and impact, perhaps through the medium of regular end-of-project completion reports. Statistical reporting had been a problem in the past, and although matters seemed to be improving, standards for most of the period had been unacceptable. The absence of a single, annual report on all aid from the EU to developing countries was a major omission.

Conclusions

Drawing the analysis together, the study of European aid to Ethiopia showed both strengths and weaknesses. An overriding impression, however, confirmed in focus group discussions, was of an aid programme that was bigger than the capacity to manage it, a problem of not cutting the coat according to the cloth. As one commentator put it, 'the EU's eyes are bigger than its stomach' (IDS and IDR, 1996, p. 107).

There are seven main ways, however, in which the programme can be improved. These are listed in Table 8.3. Some of these are Ethiopia-specific, but mostly they refer to the policy, planning, procedures, staffing and management of the European aid system as a whole. The report contains some 90 separate recommendations on these matters: budget lines to be eliminated or amalgamated; a policy manual to be prepared; a procedure for unified country strategies to be introduced; delegations to have budgets under their own control for policy analysis and programme development; the ceiling for local approval of projects to be raised from the present level of ECU 60 000; a task force to be set up to review reporting procedures; local professionals to be appointed to Delegations; and so on.

In practical terms, the evaluation concluded that the EU faced a clear choice in Ethiopia between two different strategies. One was to opt for an 'objective-driven strategy' and to tackle the problems listed in Table 8.3. The other was to 'cut the coat according to the cloth'. This would mean maximising the return to the scarce resource, which in the opinion of the evaluation team was 'professional staff time to plan, manage, monitor and evaluate an aid programme characterized by unusually great diversity and complexity' (IDS and IDR, 1996, p. 111). The strategy would involve maximising disbursement per unit of professional input, which would bias the programme to large-scale resource transfers like programme aid and large infrastructure projects, at the expense of impact on poverty, food security and other EU objectives. Clearly, an objective-driven strategy was preferable.

Table 8.3   Improving the EU aid programme in Ethiopia: 7 key issues

---

1. Simplifying and focusing the range of aid instruments.
2. Strengthening strategic planning at the country level, especially with respect to integration of instruments.
3. Improving macro-economic and sectoral policy analysis and policy dialogue (with Government and other partners).
4. Reinforcing the project cycle, leading to better project preparation and supervision.
5. Decentralising and simplifying aid administration.
6. Improving standards of reporting.
7. Better deployment of human resources, especially support for professional staff.

CONCLUSION

We started with the question 'Does European Aid Work?', and with the supposition that there might be particular advantages in terms of economies of scale or political conditionality that would justify an enlargement of EU aid at the expense of national action. The Ethiopia study allows two sorts of answers to the over-arching question about the effects of aid.

First, the study shows that some, perhaps most, European aid has 'worked', in the sense of achieving its short-term objectives; but, equally, that some has not. This answer needs to be understood as a historical judgement on a period during which the programme has evolved substantially and in which Ethiopia presented peculiar problems and

difficulties. There is certainly evidence that the quality of the programme has improved over time.

Secondly, however, further improvement is possible, and needed, if
the EU is to reach the target of an objective-driven strategy. The results
of the evaluation and the comments of the focus group discussions held
in Addis Ababa coincide in the finding that the capacity of the EU to
implement an aid programme falls some way below its capacity to agree an
over-arching aid framework and establish appropriate aid instruments.
In the focus group discussions, the EU was praised for the overall quality
of the aid framework provided by the Lomé Convention, for the range of
aid instruments at its disposal, and for providing aid in grant form. However, it was seen to compare poorly with some other donors in policy
analysis, project preparation, delegation of authority to the field, speed
and flexibility of procedures, and staffing levels. The seven-point programme in Table 8.3 reflects these concerns.

Seen in this light, the question of whether EU aid is 'better' or 'worse'
than bilateral programmes is the wrong question. Some of it is undoubtedly better; some undoubtedly worse. More accurately, the best of EU
aid is certainly better than the worst of bilateral aid; and the best of bilateral aid is certainly better than the worst of EU aid. For example, sacrificing commercially motivated aid like the infamous Pergau Dam in
favour of a sound project like Ethiopia's Amarti river diversion would
improve overall quality; but sacrificing a good bilateral rural development project to fund, say, more EU dairy aid, would reduce it.

Thus, the question about transferring resources from national programmes to the EU is actually much more interesting than simply one
about transferring resources willy-nilly from one budget to another. Instead, the question needs to be framed in terms of what will be cut on one
side, and what will be increased on the other. This discussion has yet to
take place.

At the same time, both maximalists and minimalists have an interest in
improving the quality of EU aid, along the lines set out in Table 8.3.
Some of the changes are already underway, as indicated above. However, the package is not complete. EU aid could be much better than it
already is. I have argued elsewhere (Maxwell, 1996) that the underlying
problems are political in nature, reflecting sins of omission and sins of
commission in the political arena. For example, the multiplicity of budget lines, which so complicates the administration of EU aid, probably
results from attempts at ear-marking by the European Parliament.
Similarly, the chronic under-staffing of the EU aid administration partly
reflects expenditure limits imposed by the member states (only partly,

because many problems could be solved by appointing more professional, local staff within existing budgets). Perhaps the current evaluation of
aid to the ACP will offer a vehicle for the resolution of these problems.
Or is a political initiative needed, like a European Enquiry into EU aid?

Finally, does any of this help us to adjudicate between maximalists and
minimalists? On some issues, the Ethiopia study is silent. For example, it
cannot be used to illuminate the question of whether aid to Asia, say, or
the Mediterranean, would be better framed in a Lomé-type framework.
Nor did the Ethiopia study deal with trade. On other issues, however, it is
possible to extrapolate – allowing, of course, for the particularities of the
Ethiopian case.

On contractuality and partnership, the study gives comfort if anything
to the minimalists. It eloquently supports the case against the automaticity of aid, showing how much the quality of the programme improved
when automaticity began to be eroded in Lomé III. In the focus group
discussions, recipients said they valued an explicit and negotiated aid
framework and a guaranteed flow of funds. On the first, there is no real
reason why an aid framework, setting out priorities and defining policies,
should be couched in the form of an international treaty; other donors
have frameworks without treaties. On the other hand, this is not the
same as a 'negotiated' framework, and many observers see value in the
apparatus of ACP institutions that has been created to negotiate successive Lomé agreements – even though the scope for real negotiation has
been progressively eroded. The political case for the continuation of
Lomé institutions may be stronger than the instrumental case. The real
benefits need to be debated, however. On the flow-of-funds question, a
guaranteed flow, whatever the state of domestic economic policy or the
human rights position of the recipient country, is clearly, and rightly
these days, too much to hope for. However, recipients also have a right to
be protected against back-sliding by donors (Maxwell and Riddell, 1998).

On finance, the Ethiopia study provides strong support for a unified
budgeting system, with one set of procedures and one mechanism for accountability. It does not particularly favour the EDF over the budget or
vice-versa, though it does note that historically EDF proposals and
reporting standards were generally higher than for budget-line items
(especially food aid). This may comfort the maximalists.

On the scope of the programme, the study provides evidence that
there are potential economies of scale in bringing European aid together
under a single umbrella with a range of possible instruments, not least in
the scope for policy dialogue. It was notable that many donors, including
some of the heavyweight players in Ethiopia, were anxious that the EU

should not continue to punch below its weight, and that it should play a better-informed and more active part in policy dialogue. However, the EU's potential has not always been fulfilled, and the study suggests that the Commission needs both more resources and a greater focus on country-level planning if it is to be realised. Comfort here again for the maximalists.

On political accountability, the study is neutral, but identifies serious problems in the sphere of reporting, both at country level, and more generally. This suggests that improving the structures of accountability may be less important than improving the content. Whoever controls European aid, however, the Ethiopian study also provides strong support for less intervention from outside, whether in the form of the European Parliament insisting on new budget lines, or the Member States insisting on project approval in a network of Development Council committees. Decentralisation and greater autonomy of decision-making should be the watchwords of any reform of governance of European aid.

Last but not least, administration emerges from the Ethiopia study as the Achilles heel of European aid. If this is true for an aid programme in Ethiopia serviced largely by one Directorate General, how much more true must it be for the multiplicity of structures serving the totality of developing countries. A single, semi-autonomous European Development Agency begins to look very attractive.

Notes

1. Source: DAC 1995. The figure is for 1994, up from $US 1.4 bn in 1983/84. The figure for 1993 was $US 3.9 bn.
2. Crawford (1996) and Lister (1997) review the mid-term review process and discuss the increasing conditionality of EU aid. The financial settlement agreed for EDF 8, covering the period 1996–2000, was 12 967 million ECU, to which should be added 1658 MECU of resources from the European Investment Bank. This was no increase in real terms, despite the accession since EDF 7 of 3 new EU members (Randel and German (eds) 1996, p. 209).
3. For example, Stevens, 1996; ECDPM, 1996; Eurostep, 1996.
4. I have described them elsewhere (Maxwell, 1993) as the 'Fattypuff' and 'Thinnifer' visions of EU aid.
5. DANIDA, 1991; Cox *et al.*, 1995.
6. Apart from the introduction of Structural Adjustment Support, Lomé IV also saw the innovation of programme aid within the National Indicative Programme, in the form of Sectoral and General Import Programmes.

7. The text of this section is an abridged and edited version of the relevant section of the summary of IDS and IDR, 1996.
8. The extent of the 'room for manoeuvre' is debateable, however. In the case of Uganda under Amin, Lister (1988) has argued that the EU went through the motions of negotiating and approving aid programmes, but then delayed actual disbursement until the human rights position had improved.

References

Berg, E. (1993) *Rethinking Technical Assistance and Capacity Building in Africa*, New York: UNDP.

Cassen, R. and Associates (1994) *Does Aid Work?*, 2nd edition, Oxford University Press.

Cox, A., J. Healey and A. Koning (1995) *European Union Aid Agencies: Comparative Management and Effectiveness*, 2 vols, London and Maastricht: ODI/ECDPM.

Crawford, G. (1996) 'Whither Lomé? The Mid-term Review and the Decline of Partnership', Paper presented at the European Development Policy Study Group, Development Studies Association Conference, University of Reading, 18–20 September 1996.

DAC (1995) *Development Cooperation: Efforts and Policies of the Members of the Development Assistance Committee, 1995 Report*, Paris: OECD.

DANIDA (1991) *Effectiveness of Multilateral Agencies at Country Level: European Communities in Kenya and Sudan*, prepared for DANIDA by COWIconsult Copenhagan: Danida.

European Commission (1996) *Green Paper on Relations Between the European Union and the ACP: Challenges and Options for a New Relationship*, Brussels: European Commission.

ECDPM (1996) 'Beyond Lomé IV: Exploring Options for Future ACP–EU Cooperation', *Policy Management Report*, No. 6, European Centre for Development Policy Management, Maastricht, October.

EUROSTEP (1996) *Partnership 2000: A Eurostep Approach*, Mimeo, Eurostep, Brussels, September.

Fukuda-Parr, S. (1995) 'Redefining Technical Cooperation: Challenge for the UN, or Let's Dump the Technical Cooperation Mandate' in *IDS Bulletin*, 26:4, October.

IDS and IDR (1996) *An Evaluation of Development Cooperation Between the European Union and Ethiopia, 1976–1994*, 7 vols, Institute of Development Studies, University of Sussex, and Institute of Development Research, University of Addis Ababa, June.

Lister, M.R. (1997)*The European Union and the South*, London: Routledge.

Lister, M.R. (1988) *The European Community and the Developing World*, Aldershot: Avebury.

Maxwell, S. (1993) 'Fattypuffs and Thinifers in the Debate about European Aid', in House of Lords, Select Committee on the European Communities, *EC Development Aid*, HL Paper 86, HMSO, May.

Maxwell, S. (1996) 'The Reform of European Aid: A Proposal', mimeo, July.

Maxwell, S. (1997) 'The Use of Matrix Scoring to Identify Systemic Issues in Country Programme Evaluations: The Case of EC/EU Aid to Ethiopia', *Development in Practice*, Vol. 7, No. 4.

Maxwell, S. and R. Riddell (1998) '(Conditionality or Contrast? Perspectives on Partnership in Development', *Journal of International Development* (forthcoming).

Mosley, P., and J. Hudson (1995) 'Aid Effectiveness: A Study of the Effectiveness of Overseas Aid in the Main Countries Receiving ODA Assistance', Mimeo, November.

Norway (1993) *Evaluation of Development Assistance: Handbook for Evaluators and Managers*, Royal Ministry of Foreign Affairs.

OECD (1992) *Principles for Evaluation of Development Assistance*, Paris: Organisation for Economic Cooperation and Development.

Overseas Development Institute (1995) 'EU Aid Post-Maastricht: Fifteen into One?', *Briefing Paper*, ODI, London, April.

Price Waterhouse (1992) *Study of the Causes of Delay in the Implementation of Financial and Technical Cooperation*, Brussels: Report to the European Commission.

Randel, J., and T. German (eds) (1996) *The Reality of Aid: An Independent Review of International Aid*, London: ICVA and Eurostep, Earthscan.

Stevens, C. (1996) 'Globalisation and Differentiation in EU Development Policy', Paper to Partnership 2000 Reflection Group, mimeo, Institute of Development Studies, University of Sussex.

White, H. (1992) 'The Macroeconomic Impact of Development Aid: A Critical Survey', in *Journal of Development Studies*, Vol. 28.

White, H. (1995) 'How Much Aid is Used for Poverty Reduction?' in *IDS Bulletin*, 27:1, January.

White, H, and J. Toye (eds) (1996) 'Evaluating Programme Aid', *IDS Bulletin*, 27:4, October.

9 Reform in the British and European Community Aid Programmes: Implications for the Pacific Countries[*]

Adrian Hewitt (UK, EU, Pacific)

INTRODUCTION

F35 019

In late 1996, the politician holding the recently-downgraded post of French Aid and Cooperation Minister, M. Jacques Godfrain, was observed extracting his foot from his mouth. He had the temerity to observe, during the visit of US Secretary of State Warren Christopher to Mali and subsequently to South Africa, that 'the United States was only interested in Africa in the run-up to Presidential elections'.[1] To the world outside, it seemed that America was doing rather more. Not only was it forging alliances in West and South Africa, the US was establishing relationships with a new generation of governments in the Great Lakes region and Central Africa in particular, while France appeared unhappily tied to old clientelisms. European foreign policy in the region, moreover, was inchoate because of differences between France and most of the other EU member states.

Godfrain's remark was marginally less insulting than the old chestnut we all heard in the first year of the Clinton presidency: 'US foreign policy would not be as bad as this if Warren Christopher were still alive'. But it provoked an equally robust response from Mr Christopher who demanded an apology from the French government and then went on to castigate France for running an old-fashioned, paternalistic and divisive African policy based on nineteenth-century notions of spheres of influence.[2]

This may sound a rather depressing and counterproductive way of starting a paper about UK and European aid – especially one focused on the Pacific. But it is not. First, this incident proved that Africa *matters*; even Mali matters to the superpowers, even after the end of the Cold

---

[*] This paper draws on helpful discussions held with the Fiji Economics Association on 4 June 1996, when the author gave a public lecture on the same subject.

119

War. By extension, poor developing countries matter and the African, Caribbean and Pacific (ACP) Group comprises a majority of these by number.

Secondly, a word of caution. France's aid and cooperation policy is the policy on which Europe's is based. Even though the latter is evolving, no one can gainsay this historic fact, which relates to Part IV of the Treaty of Rome. And thirdly, the Africa we are talking about is the prime constituent part of the ACP (even South Africa has been given associate status within it): not only would it be wrong to think that the P (the Pacific) would gain any particular advantages from seceding from the A and the C (especially the A, Africa), but the same above-rule applies: the *reason* why Europe in 1973–5 singled out the ACP for special treatment (and not, say, the other Member States' ex-colonies such as India, Bangladesh, Malaysia and Indonesia, where the British and the Dutch might have made a stronger case) was because France had a foothold in each of these three areas. Indeed it continues to have overseas departments and dependent territories, DOM–TOM, the very target of the first EDF, in each of these three areas – in the Caribbean and the Pacific as well as off the east coast of Africa where the Comorian island of Anjouan is lately clamouring to return to the French dependency status enjoyed by Mayotte or Réunion.

One last reason for my focusing on the Pacific region was that when this conference was being organised, this session was to have one paper on Africa and another on the Caribbean. Moreover, a recent series of World Bank country studies had compared the economic performance of the Pacific islands unfavourably with that of island states in the Caribbean, despite allegedly similar levels of aid.[3] My paper was to be complementary, even if many would judge the Pacific to be of lesser importance to the ACP and to the EU. But Cinderella can still go to the ball (even if her Caribbean partner is no longer here!), so let us proceed.

THE ARGUMENT

The argument is the following. The Pacific – the South Pacific nations – matters because of the countries' intrinsic merit, their position also on the Pacific rim, because of the ties of history and culture and because they – Papua New Guinea, Fiji, Solomon Islands, Vanuatu, Tonga, Tuvalu, Kiribati and Samoa – are ACP states with their European acquis. Britain is both withdrawing from the Pacific and reforming its (bilateral) aid in a direction which will not in any case benefit the Pacific states.

But one of the reasons for doing this is because of (bilateral) spending constraints, as evidenced by the Fundamental Expenditure Review (FER) as well as annual budget cuts. One of the reasons for the cuts, and indeed for the FER (if the House of Commons Foreign Affairs Committee is to be believed) is pressure on the bilateral aid budget from the UK's European aid obligations. Yet in the Pacific, which are the donors expanding their aid programmes? Not Australia, hardly Japan and certainly not Britain: only the European Union (although with some difficulties in spending it) and France. I shall go into the reason why France is expanding later – it is a matter of raw politics and Chiraquien reaction after the débâcle of the last Mururoa nuclear tests. But there is one more, crucial reason why such a shift in aid policy and competencies is interesting to us as well as to the Pacific countries concerned, and if we have not spotted it, we would have been alerted to it by none other than Sir James Goldsmith in his Referendum Party manifesto:

So when, according to the [Maastricht] Treaty [on European Union] can subsidiarity be applied? The answer is when it is deemed that a particular action cannot be carried out 'sufficiently' well at the national level and that, I quote, it can be better achieved by the Community.[4]

The case I have set out above, and for which I offer a few more details below – but which I trust can still be challenged, FER, SMR[5] and FAC reports notwithstanding – looks suspiciously like a case of the UK exiting from one of the ACP regions because it feels it can no longer 'sufficiently' accomplish its (development assistance) task and concedes that the EC can somehow do it 'better'. If this is the case, then history and the treaties tell us that such powers, including spending powers, cannot be clawed back. And anyway, were the Pacific nations asked which they preferred, which gave them the best value-for-money?

CHANGES IN THE UK AID PROGRAMME

For the South Pacific, the UK's aid policy has provided a double-whammy over the past year. First in 1995 was the Pacific Aid Review which recommended withdrawal from virtually all the countries in the region. Papua New Guinea had not had capital aid, Fiji's was to be phased out, and there were (political) difficulties with spending it in Solomon Islands; the other countries were deemed either too small or too rich (or both – in fact the World Bank classifies their populations as living in 'subsistence affluence' and now notes problems of urban poverty). Then the 1996 ODA/FCO Fundamental Expenditure Review recommended a slimming down of the UK bilateral aid programme just to sub-Saharan Africa and a few named South Asian countries. Although this was not fully accepted by ministers, it looks as if the Pacific still has lost out; this was consolidated in budget cuts (in Table 9.1 I reproduce the pattern in 1995–6 with plans for the next three years[6]) which shows that the Pacific is to suffer the biggest cuts of all, down to a mere £3 million in (planned) 1998–9.

Note, however, not only that the multilateral share and amount overtakes the bilateral share and amount in that just-past 1995–6 financial year (£1.132m against £1.125m, with a much larger disparity by 1998–9), but also that it is Britain's European aid contributions, and specifically those to the EU budgetised programmes, rather than to the EDF (which benefits the ACP directly) which are the main cause of the rising disparity. So UK aid spending has been doubly redirected away from the Pacific. Note too that this is only raw financial (budgetary) data: no criteria of aid effectiveness or value-for-money have yet been applied.

In mitigation, it must be said that for some Pacific ACP countries (though not the poorest) it is not aid, whether Member State or European Union, which is the most valuable, but the preferential trade arrangements enjoyed under the Sugar Protocol. Scott MacDonald has calculated[7] this has been worth up to $50m per year for Fiji, making these aid numbers pale into insignificance, as the aid itself will shortly do. Whereas, however, the Sugar Protocol itself will outlast the Lomé Convention (which expires in 2000), there is no guarantee that Fiji will enjoy preferential sugar prices which generate such sums into the future. (The costs are not borne by the aid budget in this case, but by consumers.)

The 'double whammy' affects the Pacific in another way, because the new UK aid policies just happen not to be Pacific-friendly. Let me explain. My text is that of the 1996 Fundamental Expenditure Review (FER).

Thanks to the FER, the ODA (and its programme) now has four aims. Her Majesty's Government has also in the review apparently accepted the principle of bilateral country concentration (although Aim 4 broadens out the approach towards a multilateral reach, and helpfully addresses development questions well beyond aid), which members of the Independent Group on British Aid urged upon it – together with poverty-focus and aid-untying – as long ago as 1982.[8] The largest 20 recipients now enjoy 69 per cent of UK aid and that proportion is to increase until the 20 countries enjoy just so much of the aid programme as ministers finally determine (the matter is in dispute, although many read the FER as implying a figure as high as 90–100 per cent). What is certain is that no South Pacific country is in this charmed circle.[9]

Aim 1 is to encourage sound development policies, efficient markets and good government. Ghana and Uganda are cited as paragons. Despite some back-sliding on the political front, the Pacific nations are too good to qualify for aid under Aim 1.

Aim 2 is to achieve better education and health and to widen opportunities, especially for women. Again, the Pacific has been rather too progressive to qualify for aid on this score – such is 'moral hazard'. However, the Pacific countries do qualify from a residual UK regional aid programme in education and 'governance' (see again Note 9), especially in the legal/administrative domain.

Aim 3 is to enhance productive capacity and to conserve the environment. (After the unexpected – to President Chirac – reaction throughout the region to the Mururoa atomic tests, the French governments *expanded* its bilateral aid programme to the region in order to help conserve the environment, and restore some political credibility.) The UK position is different. Despite environmental fragility, serious logging scams and enormous productive potential in the region, aid is being withdrawn.

Aim 4 is to promote international development policies and enhance the effectiveness of multilateral development institutions. This is precisely the aim which, if accomplished, goes beyond aid. But within this aim, anything concerning trade (at least, trade in goods) is within the policy remit of the EU. And since both the World Bank and the Asian Development Bank (of which the UK is a full member) too regard their South Pacific members as rather too small for concerted policy attention, on the 'multilateral' front it is only the EU, and for aid purposes the EDF, to which this broadening-out of UK aid policy to multilateralism applies, both as regards aid and trade. And that too is why the UK appears to have (prematurely) applied the doctrine of subsidiarity and handed over operations to the EU.

AUSTRALIAN AID

The South Pacific is Australia's 'near abroad', even if the distances can sometimes be vast and although in practical terms the weight of Indonesia and the continental countries of Asia is dominant for foreign-policy purposes. It would be wrong, though, to see Australia's position as entirely the reverse of that of Europe: Australia too has international

Table 9.1   UK aid: cash plans, 1993–94 to 1998–99 (£m)

	1993–94 (outturn)	1994–95 (outturn)	1995–96 (estimated)	1996–97 (plans)	1997–98 (plans)	1998–99 (plans)	Trend
Aid Resources available for allocation (excluding pensions and GEF)	2107	2258	2256	2155	2201	2270	Flat
ALLOCATION							
Bilateral Country programmes							
Africa (including Middle East)	268	261	276	348	314	328	
Asia	192	205	233	254	247	252	
Pacific	12	10	8	6	4	3	Falling Fast
Latin America	26	24	24	25	24	20	
Caribbean	55	43	51	48	43	38	
Central/East Europe & Central Asia	63	76	85	82	77	76	
Other Bilateral							
Aid and Trade Provision	85	67	77	–	–	–	
British Council	31	34	34	33	29	26	
Commonwealth Development Corporation	75	33	46	16	23	21	
Emergency aid & Food Aid	181	209	102	65	48	34	

Other	182	184	189	170	162	157	
TOTAL BILATERAL	1170	1146	1125	1047	971	954	Decreasing
Multilateral:							
EU Budgetised Programmes	325	347	480	578	632	714	Increasing rapidly
European Development Fund	172	243	247	225	280	252	Stable since 1994
World Bank/IMF	249	318	236	194	197	210	
Other Banks and Funds	77	74	69	58	71	71	
United Nations	95	77	56	67	62	54	
Emergency Aid	31	17	17	7	7	7	
Other Multilateral	21	25	27	17	15	16	
TOTAL MULTILATERAL	970	1101	1132	1147	1265	1324	Increasing

Source: FCO/ODA Departmental Report, 1996.

treaty obligations in the region, notably those covering aid commitments to Papua New Guinea, and its governments can sometimes be equivocal about aid. As a result, Papua New Guinea continues to be by far the largest recipient of Australian aid (A$ 337m in 1995/6, or some US$250m), with Indonesia in second place at A$130m. Fiji receives about A$20m, while the other South Pacific island countries are allocated about A$12m each (except for the smallest – Kiribati, Tuvalu and Nauru – which get much less). Regional integration is also encouraged with aid.

The new Coalition Government has however announced substantial cuts in the aid programme, from which the South Pacific will not be insulated. Initially, the cuts will total 10 per cent (about A$150m in real terms), bringing Australia's ODA : GNP ratio down from 0.34 per cent to 0.29 per cent. But wider changes may be afoot.

Australia's Foreign Minister, Alexander Downer, has claimed domestic budget stringency as the reason for the overseas aid cut: 'Australia must put its own economic house in order first before it can achieve higher aid levels in future'.[10] However, he too has called for a fundamental review of aid policy, to be led by Paul Simons, and the leaking of an Australian Government report in July 1997 at a meeting of Pacific Island Economic Ministers (from which, it must be said, Mr Downer quickly distanced himself) did little to encourage South Pacific governments, since the report described their countries without exception as corrupt and mismanaged. Individual Pacific leaders were categorized as 'a belligerent drunk', 'arrogant and brutal' and 'Mr 10 per cent', while neighbouring New Zealand and Malaysia were deemed to be countering Australian policy at every turn. The report succeeded, in the words of former foreign minister Gareth Evans, in 'offending fifteen countries in one go'.[11] It does not augur well for future Australian aid policy in the region.

Of course, the attitudes and public utterances of Australian politicians – whether in government or opposition – are more robust than those of Europeans, especially when dealing with the Pacific. Treaty commitments will mean that aid to Papua New Guinea is maintained, although it is now shifting from budgetary to more closely-controlled programme aid (the latter exceeded 50 per cent for the first time in 1996); similarly the island economies will receive Australian aid which is more focused on public sector management and economic policy reform in the future. None the less, 10 per cent cuts, in an aid programme which is so dominant, if continued, would begin to reflect the disengagement of other donors from the region. This would put under the spotlight the programmes of residual donors which are not cutting back, such as the European Union, to which we now turn.

EUROPEAN COMMUNITY AID

The EU's position could hardly be more different. There is no budgetary stress – see Table 9.1 (indeed, the EDF itself is still maintained as an ex-tra-budgetary account, and has been replenished for another five years at 13.4 billion ecus, with the UK liable for 12.75 per cent). The European Commission's 1997 Green Paper on the Future of EU–ACP relations, while seeming to advocate some degree of differentiation in treatment of the ACP, does not propose dropping any part of the Group.

Nonetheless, the ACP have some concerns (and the Pacific nations within the Group have some legitimate special preoccupations). The ACP are rightly worried about the continuing nature of their 1975-vintage relationship with the EU (which, in fact, harks back to France's policy in the last three years before its African colonies gained independence). They have a lot to lose – their 'acquis' in fact:

- 'equal' partnership;
- automatic entitlement to aid;
- 'no-strings' wider procurement; and
- long-term, treaty-based aid and trade concessions.

But these are all mid-1970s ideas – there is nothing of the conditionality which now governs donor relationships or the globalisation which is the essential backdrop to both trade and foreign investment here. Addition-ally, the ACP are concerned that Europe is becoming more interested in *its* 'near-abroad' – Eastern European candidate states, the Balkans, Rus-sia and the Caucasus, and the Southern Mediterranean – than the ACP, especially far-flung bits of it like the Pacific.

The economic relationship is still rather fragile. Europe takes one-fifth of Pacific ACP exports but supplies only one-tenth of imports, yet Europe's aid provision (Member State and Commission-administered aid combined) is 23 per cent overall, the rising share being that of the EC within this. Investments have not shifted quickly enough from – essen-tially protected – agricultural raw material production into sectors such as services, in which small island economies in an already-remote region can demonstrate comparative advantage by capitalising on the new tech-nologies. The European Commission's own justification of the Pacific ACP link, though a model of European political correctness by its refer-ence to a wide range of European voyages and voyagers of discovery, is uncomfortably nostalgic; in a more global sense, it succeeds in being breath-takingly politically incorrect:

Bougainville, Cook, Torres, Santa Isabel, Tasmania, Finschhafen, Pitcairn…the map of the South Pacific area is a store of nostalgic reminders of associations with Europe going back to the eighteenth and nineteenth centuries and earlier. After the early seafarers came merchantmen and planters, then missionaries and finally [sic] the administrators of the colonial era, which was to last for nearly a hundred years.[12]

Yet what the EU does still offer is a buoyant aid programme and a formal negotiating process with regional privileges. The Pacific ACP states would be unwise to forgo these advantages out of pique for a donor's unreconstructed political attitudes – for they might find the same on offer from their near-neighbours too.

Meanwhile, it can hardly be said that the South Pacific has got its act together. Only PNG managed to join Asia-Pacific Economic Cooperation (APEC) before the US imposed the moratorium on new members. Not a single other ACP state in the Pacific region was smart enough to join the Asia-*Pacific* Economic Cooperation in time. They are concerned too that their privileges on bananas, on Stabex drawings and even on sugar will be withdrawn – although Fiji at least is being more rational about addressing cost-of-production questions than some Caribbean producers, and preparing itself for the time when it has to compete on world markets without guaranteed European access. Although, or possibly because, these nations have a 'Pacific way' of resolving their problems and dealing with foreigners, they have been loath to point out that, for example, Solomon Islands has been discriminated against by the EU in being prevented from drawing down Stabex funds to which it is entitled under the terms of the Convention, when numerous African ACP countries, committing much more serious misdemeanours, have been allowed their Stabex allocations. But they are also aware of an attitude – which comes as much from within local, EU Delegations, often staffed by 'Old Africa Hands', as from the posts of the European Member States – to the effect that the Pacific does not 'belong' in the ACP and it is not 'entitled' to EU aid and trade privileges in the way that Africa is. This argument, it must be said, is often couched in terms of history (and geography!), rather than being deployed as an explanation of the Pacific's relative prosperity, democracy and lack of poverty and need. But the Pacific governments are now concerned that they do not 'belong' in the ACP, and perhaps never did belong.

Let me conclude by addressing this very argument. I do this by issuing a straight denial. The South Pacific nations are in Lomé for the same reason that the sub-Saharan African states are ACP. They are successor states of countries which had an attachment to an EEC Member State. This is not just the UK, although Britain negotiated the valuable Sugar Protocol at least partly on behalf of Fiji, but particularly because of France, which still has important possessions in the region[13] including the nickel-rich island of New Caledonia – second in size only to Papua New Guinea and itself enjoying EDF aid as well as the trade preferences which come to all DOM/TOM and special-status French possessions – and French Polynesia. These countries are not so poor as most African ACP countries (though they are poorer than all the Caribbean save Haiti and Guyana); but nor are they so close to Europe for their trade as these other two ACP areas. They seem to be unfairly discriminated against, even if their relative prosperity is the clinching factor for the withdrawal of aid.

Even under a new British Government's policy of concentrating aid on the poorest countries and liquidating its last dependencies, I have yet to be convinced that it is in either Britain's or the EU's overall develop-ment-policy interest to withdraw support entirely from those regions of the developing world which are doing rather well economically or polit-ically, but which still remain vulnerable: not only is there always more room for improvement – and room to absorb aid effectively – but also there is a very good developmental and self-interested reason for donors such as the UK *and* the EU to play to their partners' strengths. These Pa-cific ACP members are small, often well-managed trading nations in the wide and resource-rich Pacific Ocean and on the edge (or 'rim') of the most buoyant part of the world economy, and we here in Europe would be unwise to exit just now. It was over 20 years ago that a famous UK White Paper asserted 'We believe that the Community should have a worldwide aid policy'.[14] And to end on a much more parochial point, if the UK effectively exits because it cuts back its aid programme there, this is tantamount to conceding subsidiarity to an EU operation which has yet to be proved – or deemed in the eyes of the Pacific governments – to be superior.

Notes

1.   *Le Monde*, 15 October 1996.
2.   *Le Monde*, 16 October 1996.
3.   *Towards Higher Growth in Pacific Island Economies: Lessons form the 1980s*. World Bank, 1991; *Pacific Island Economies: Towards Efficient and*

Sustainable Growth. World Bank, 1993; *Pacific Island Economies: Building a Resilient Economic Base for the Twenty-First Century*. World Bank, 1995.

4. 'Who Governs Britain?' published by the Referendum Party, 1996, p. 7.
5. One of the implications of the Senior Management Review which followed a regional aid review was to wind down the UK bilateral aid presence in the form of aid management offices in the Pacific Islands. The EU maintains two delegations and four offices in the Pacific ACP countries.
6. Table 9.1 is adapted from the 1996 FCO/ODA Departmental Report.
7. Scott MacDonald in 'Reform of the EU's Sugar Policies and the ACP countries' *Development Policy Review*, No. 2, 1996.
8. *Real Aid: A Strategy for Britain*, IGBA, 1982. Both Simon Maxwell, who is giving the Ethiopia paper (the 'A' of ACP), and the present author, were founder-members of IGBA.
9. A British Embassy Press Release (Suva, Fiji) dated 4 June 1996 states: 'Contrary to recent reporting, the UK is not abandoning the South Pacific nor has the UK Government's interest in the region disappeared. It is however true that the consequence of having to channel more of our aid through multilateral agencies (*sic*) means that bilateral resources for the Pacific are scarcer'. The paper goes on to say that this effectively means *regional* aid only ('the bilateral programme to Fiji has been phased out and there will be no new commitments') and then only in the areas of education and 'good governance'.

    The speech by Foreign Minister of State Jeremy Hanley MP to the Pacific Islands Society, the Commonwealth Trust and the British Friends of Vanuatu, at the Royal Overseas League on 24 January 1996, even has a section entitled 'Pulling out'; part of the text reads: 'We will also maintain a sizeable programme of bilateral aid. But the trend towards multilateral aid, inevitably, I am afraid, means on this front that the news is less good... I had to speak of future reductions... Too often in recent years, too much of our aid budget for the Pacific has gone unspent because we have been unable to agree programmes with government'. Full text published in *Britain in Fiji* (DTI/FCO Overseas Trade Services) No. 8, April 1996.
10. *Australia's Overseas Aid Program 1996–97*, circulated by Hon. Alexander Downer MP, 20 August 1996. Canberra: Australian Government Publishing Service.
11. BBC World Service 20 July 1997.
12. European Commission: *The South Pacific and the European Union*. Brussels, June 1996.
13. Three of the four European dependencies draw EDF aid: New Caledonia, French Polynesia and the Wallis and Futuna Islands. The small British dependent territory of Pitcairn does not.
14. *The Changing Emphasis in British Aid Policies: More Help for the Poorest*, Command 6270, HMSO, 1975, p. 54.

10 Human Rights and Democracy in EU Development Co-operation: Towards Fair and Equal Treatment[*]

Gordon Crawford

INTRODUCTION

A striking innovation in EU development co-operation policy in the 1990s has been the promotion of human rights and democracy. This objective was similarly declared by many other aid donors at this time, including most EU member states. Such policies are in contrast to Cold War practices when donor governments, West and East, were willing to reward compliant regimes with economic support regardless of their authoritarianism or treatment of domestic populations.

Whilst a welcome shift from such practices, the recent policy agenda is not itself unproblematic. The incorporation of the principles of human rights and democracy have generally not in themselves been a contentious issue for most aid recipient states, with the notable exception of ASEAN members.[1] The manner of policy implementation has sparked concerns, however. For example, the practice of unilateral suspension of countries from the Lomé Convention was opposed by the ACP Group in the recent mid-term review of Lomé IV.[2] The likelihood of consistent application of policy has also been doubted by a number of commentators on 'political conditionality'.[3] This is not surprising, given how a previous attempt at a human rights linkage by the US Congress during the Carter presidency was characterised by inconsistency.[4] Moreover, the broader experience of judgements of human rights performance during

* The author wishes to acknowledge the grant received from the UK Economic and Social Research Council that facilitated this research, and to thank both Viki Harvey for initial assistance in gathering information on EU aid sanctions and David Beetham for helpful comments on the draft.

the Cold War years was one of selectivity and lack of objectivity, condemning the poor records of opponents whilst overlooking that of allies.[5]
Perhaps with that historical experience in mind, the UN Vienna Conference in 1993 declared that 'The international community must treat
human rights globally in a fair and equal manner, on the same footing,
and with the same emphasis.'[6]

This chapter examines the implementation of human rights and
democracy policies within the aid programmes provided by the European
Commission. It focuses on two policy instruments: the inclusion of
human rights and democracy clauses in development co-operation agreements; and the imposition of aid sanctions in situations of perceived
violations of human rights or reversals in the democratisation process.[7]
It assesses the application of both instruments on the criterion of consistency. It highlights some of the shortcomings in policy implementation
and suggests improvements in practices and procedures towards policy
being applied in an objective, non-selective, fair and equal manner.

The chapter is in four parts. First, it traces the evolution of policy at
EU level. In the second and third parts, it proceeds to examine and assess
the implementation of the two policy instruments: human rights and
democracy clauses, and aid-restrictive measures. Finally, it concludes by
discussing the importance of consistent application for policy legitimacy,
and offers some recommendations.

POLICY EVOLUTION

Policy in this field has arisen out of the overall development of an essen-
tially economic Community into a body with political objectives. This
process gained momentum after the events of 1989 in Central and Eastern Europe, with declarations on human rights and democracy becoming a regular feature of European Council meetings.[8] The consolidation
of this shift to explicit political aims is evident in the Maastricht Treaty
on European Union (TEU), which came into force in November 1993,
with respect for human rights made a general principle of Community
law, hence informing all its activities [Article F(2)]. In addition, with
regard to external relations and the new pillar of common foreign and
security policy (CFSP), the development and consolidation of democracy
and the rule of law, and of respect for human rights and fundamental
freedoms, was stated as a principal objective [Art. J. 1(2)].

The enhancement of these political features also found expression in
development co-operation policy. The Commission Communication of

March 1991, on 'Human Rights, Democracy and Development Co-opera-tion', felt it 'vital that human rights and democratization figure more prominently in the guidelines for co-operation policy than has hitherto been the case'. This was regarded as a significant shift for the Commis-sion, who had previously regarded their aid programme as free of polit-ical considerations, unlike those of other donors in the Cold War context, indicating that the pressure for policy change came from intergovern-mental mechanisms. The subsequent Resolution of the Council of Ministers (Development) in November 1991, on 'Human Rights, Demo-cracy and Development', made the promotion of human rights and democracy both an objective and a condition of development co-operation not only for the European Community, but also for Member States.[9] Both the Commission's proposals and the Development Council Resolution were supported by the European Parliament.[10]

Further, the aims of EU development co-operation were defined for the first time in the TEU (Title XVII, Articles 130 u–y), with political aspects given high priority, declaring 'the general objective of developing and consolidating democracy and the rule of law, and that of respecting human rights and fundamental freedoms'.[11]

The November 1991 Council Resolution was, and remains, the pivotal policy statement in this area, however. It delineated four political ele-ments as part of a larger set of requirements to achieve sustainable de-velopment: human rights, democracy, good governance and decreased military expenditure. It outlined two main policy instruments, a carrot and a stick: 'high priority' was accorded to 'a positive approach that stimu-lates respect for human rights and encourages democracy' through the provision of financial resources; yet with the warning that appropriate measures will be taken 'in the event of grave and persistent human rights violations or the serious interruption of democratic processes', up to and including suspension of co-operation agreements.[12] It also stated that 'human rights clauses will be inserted in future co-operation agree-ments'.[13] Such a clause spans the division between positive and negative measures. In itself it can act to promote human rights and democracy, whilst simultaneously serving as a means to authorise restrictive meas-ures if deemed to be violated.

This chapter limits itself to an examination and assessment of policy implementation in two respects: the inclusion of human rights and demo-cracy clauses in new co-operation agreements, and the taking of negative measures in response to alleged violations of human rights and democra-cy principles. Given constraints on length, it is not possible also to exam-ine 'positive action' in the form of projects and programmes aimed at

promoting human rights and democracy, financed either through specifically earmarked budget-lines or out of the general allocations of financial and technical assistance for each country.

HUMAN RIGHTS AND DEMOCRACY CLAUSES

Development co-operation agreements between the EU and 'third
countries' benefit from having a firm contractual basis. The EU has been
at the forefront of the inclusion of a human rights and democracy clause
as a legal instrument in development co-operation agreements, referred
to as a standard component by the mid-1990s. Increasingly such a clause
is inserted as an 'essential element', with an associated 'suspension' or
'non-performance' clause.[14] A few other countries, notably Belgium, Germany and Sweden, have begun to do likewise.[15] How has this practice
evolved? How have the clauses been applied? What have been, and remain,
the contentious issues?

Evolution

The first reference to human rights in the main body of an agreement
predated, in fact, the post-Cold War developments. Article 5 of the
fourth Lomé Convention, signed in late 1989 between the EU member
states and the group of 70 ACP states, stated that 'respect for human
rights is recognised as a basic factor of real development', with co-operation 'conceived as a contribution to the promotion of these rights'.[16] But,
despite being a significant innovation at the time, Article 5 was relatively
insubstantial in comparison with later clauses. It made no mention of
democracy, preceding both the collapse of communism in Eastern Europe
and the resurgence of democratisation movements in Africa. Further, it
did not constitute an essential element of the agreement, thus lacking a
legal basis for suspension of co-operation in the event of human rights
violations.[17] In practice, however, the Commission did unilaterally suspend co-operation in a number of instances, for example: Sudan – full
suspension in 1990; Haiti – full suspension in September 1991; Zaire –
partial freeze in January 1992; Malawi – new projects suspended from
May 1992. (See Table 10.1 for a full presentation of aid-restrictive measures.)

The process of extending the scope of human rights clauses and of
strengthening them as legal instruments, particularly after the Council
Resolution of November 1991, has involved the evolution of different

formulas. Developments have been four-fold, and can be traced through both the Commission communications on the subject[18] and the insertions of clauses in actual signed agreements.

1. The **'democratic principles' clause** extended the concerns to include respect for democratic principles as well as human rights. It was first used in 1990 in Latin America.
2. By stipulating that a human rights and democracy clause constitutes an **'essential element' clause**, the necessary legal basis for suspension of the agreement is provided. This was first introduced in 1992. [Two alternative, supplementary clauses insert a suspension mechanism which supplants the long-winded procedures of the Vienna Convention (see Note 14).]
3. The explicit **'suspension clause'** enables either Party immediately to suspend the Agreement either in whole or in part if a serious infringement of the essential provisions occurs. Known as the **'Baltic' clause**, it was first used in the agreements with the Baltic states in late 1992.
4. The general **'non-performance' or 'non-execution' clause** states in more detail the procedures to be followed in situations of alleged violations. It establishes an investigative body (known as 'the Association Council'), which seeks a mutually acceptable solution. Measures selected are to be 'those which least disturb the functioning of the Agreement', and can be the subject of consultations within the Association Council if so requested by the other Party. Immediate suspension is only envisaged in cases of 'special urgency'. Known as the **'Bulgarian' clause**, it was first used in agreements with Bulgaria and other Central and Eastern European states from 1993.

Since its inception the Bulgarian clause has become the preferred formula, with the Commission proposing in 1995 that it become a standard in all new agreements.[19] The differences between the Baltic and Bulgarian varieties are the respective degrees of harshness and flexibility. The Baltic clause is more severe, entailing immediate suspension, yet its applicability is limited to more extreme cases of gross human rights violations. The Bulgarian clause can be adapted as appropriate to a variety of circumstances, involving consulation procedures and a range of different measures. The Bulgarian clause can be criticised, however, for its relative 'softness'. The word 'suspension' is conspicuous by its absence and the emphasis is on the avoidance of negative measures. Disquiet has been expressed that this clause, almost designed not to be used, should become the standard formula.[20]

Application

The inclusion of the different formulas in signed agreements has evolved over time and also followed a regional pattern. Following the human rights clause in Lomé IV, its extension to include democratic principles occurred initially in agreements with Latin American countries. Significantly, this initiative came from the newly democratic governments in Latin America themselves who wanted the commitment from the EU that development and trade co-operation would not continue in the event of future military intervention. Thus, human rights and democracy clauses were initially included in the agreements concluded with Argentina (April 1990)[21] and Chile (December 1990),[22] followed by Uruguay (March 1992)[23] and Paraguay (October 1992).[24] The strengthening of this clause as an 'essential element', following a Council decision to this effect,[25] was first introduced in the agreement with Brazil in June 1992, then in the regional co-operation agreements with the Central American Isthmus (February 1993) and Andean Pact countries (April 1993).[26]

The first new European agreements, concluded with Hungary and Poland in December 1991, contained a reference to human rights in the Preamble only. Subsequent agreements from late 1992 onwards all contained a human rights and democracy clause as an essential element. Suspension clauses were inserted from late 1992 onwards in European agreements, and were in fact initially intended for countries only. The 'Baltic' variety was included in those with Albania (October 1992),[27] Estonia, Latvia and Lithuania (December 1992),[28] and Slovenia (July 1993),[29] and the 'Bulgarian' clause with Romania (February 1993), Bulgaria (March 1993), the Czech Republic and Slovakia (both October 1993).[30] It is arguable that the EU had the most leverage and met the least resistance in its negotiations with the new governments of Central and Eastern Europe who, like the newly civilian governments in Argentina and Chile, probably felt protected rather than threatened by such conditionality. Additionally, the EU had the greatest self-interest in ensuring the principles of human rights and democracy were upheld in this region, particularly given the expanding conflagration in ex-Yugoslavia at that time.

The inclusion of human rights and democracy clauses in agreements with Asian countries followed the same initial pattern, with a democratic principles clause included in new agreements with Mongolia (February 1992) and Macao (December 1992). In subsequent agreements this became an essential element clause, for example, India (December 1993) and Sri Lanka (May 1994). Up to 27 April 1995, no suspension clause had been incorporated into an agreement with an Asian country. Subsequently it has been inserted in agreements with Nepal and South Korea.

The revisions made during the mid-term review of Lomé IV, affecting the 70 ACP countries, were of particular significance. The outcome of the Review, signed in November 1995, has been to broaden and strengthen the human rights linkage introduced in 1989. Article 5 has been expanded to include 'democratic principles', the 'rule of law' and 'good governance' as aims of development co-operation, with all except 'good governance' becoming an 'essential element' of the Convention. A suspension mechanism has been added (Art. 366a), applied for the first time to other geographical areas outside Central and Eastern Europe. It was notable that the cooperation agreement with the government of the new South Africa, concluded in December 1994 and comparable with those already signed with the new governments in Eastern Europe, did not contain a suspension clause.

In the Mediterranean region, the co-operation agreements initially signed in the 1970s contained no provisions on human rights, and this remained unchanged in the fourth financial protocol under these agreements for 1992–6. However, the new Euro-Mediterranean Association Agreements, already signed with Tunisia, Israel and Morocco and under negotiation with the other countries, contain a human rights and democracy clause as an essential element with an associated suspension article.[31]

Consistency?

The pattern of inclusion of human rights and democracy clauses reveals a picture characterised by inconsistency. Two points could be made in mitigation, though. One is that time is required for a new and evolving practice to become established and be applied as a common formula. The other is the Commission's awareness of the issue of inconsistency and its attempt to address it. In January 1993, it noted 'the lack of consistency ... in Community agreements with non-member countries', and provided guidelines for negotiating new agreements in an attempt to ensure a more systematic approach.[32] Further, the Commission Communication of May 1995 provided standard wording for human rights clauses for all new negotiating directives,[33] subsequently adopted by the Council of Ministers.

Nevertheless, the extent to which this standard clause will in fact be applied as common practice remains uncertain, with doubts focusing on the political will of the Union. First, the standard wording applies to

negotiating directives only, with its insertion in signed agreements dependent on the outcome of negotiations with the third country. Second, and
more significantly, countries in the Asian and Mediterranean regions
throw up other, potentially conflicting, interests.

In Asia, some country agreements, originally signed in the 1970s and
1980s with no human rights provisions, continue to be rolled over on the
basis of the old agreements, with little indication of their re-negotiation.
This is most evident in the case of EU–ASEAN relations. The Trade and
Cooperation agreement between the EU and ASEAN members dates
from 1980. The EU–ASEAN ministerial meeting in 1991 decided to
revise the agreement, with negotiations commencing in 1992. Two stumb-
ling blocks emerged, however. One was the proposed insertion of a human rights clause, to which the ASEAN governments objected. The
other was the continued occupation of East Timor by Indonesia, with
Portugal unwilling to sign a new agreement with this issue unresolved.
Co-operation continues, however, under the terms of the original agreement, with discussions of a new agreement apparently shelved. It was not
even an agenda item at the 1994 Ministerial Meeting.[34]

Why has the EU failed to implement policy in a non-discriminatory
manner, despite a stated determination to do so in January 1993? It is
evident that a concern for trade and investment opportunities predomi-
nates in the EU's relations with regions of economic expansion, notably
South East Asia. The Commission's *Asia Strategy* paper stated quite
explicitly that the Union's interest 'is in the first instance primarily
economic' and of the need 'as a matter of urgency to strengthen its economic presence in Asia in order to maintain its leading role in the world
economy'.[35] In particular, the EU's relationship with ASEAN is viewed
as 'a corner stone of its dialogue with Asia'.[36] The introduction of political conditionality within a new co-operation agreement would undoubtedly meet with robust opposition from at least some ASEAN member
states, and the EU is unwilling to pose a threat to its own commercial
interests.

The EU has prioritised recently the strengthening of its relations with
the countries of North African and the Middle East, culminating with
the Barcelona declaration of the Euro-Mediterranean partnership and
the negotiation of new Association Agreements. As outlined above,
these are to include the standard human rights and democracy clause.
Yet we come up against a conundrum. The EU has demonstrated a clear
intention to strengthen its links with its Mediterranean neighbours in
pursuit of trade and security objectives, with a large increase in aid, total-
ling ECU 4.7 billion for the period 1995–9.[37] Beneficiaries of this assist-

ance include the governments of Algeria, Syria and Egypt, none noted for their commitment to the principles of human rights and democracy. (See below for mini case-studies of Algeria and Egypt.)

It is contended here that the maintenance of current aid to these three governments is in contradiction to the EU's stated human rights policies. How can new agreements be concluded, including the insertion of a human rights and democracy clause, with governments that show such disrespect for those very principles? Would they not require immediate suspension? It seems likely that the EU will seek somehow to square the human rights circle in order not to jeopardise these agreements.[38] The watchdog role of the European Parliament, with its veto powers over new agreements, will be critical.

RESTRICTIVE MEASURES

Aid sanctions 1990–95

A rising scale of restrictive measures has been identified by the Commission in response to perceived human rights abuses or interruptions in the democratization process, ranging from confidential démarches to full suspension of co-operation. This includes some measures (for example, démarches, deferment of signatures to implement co-operation) which by their nature are not publicly transparent.

From information in the public domain a survey was undertaken of the aid sanctions implemented globally by the EU on human rights and democracy grounds during the period 1990 to early 1996. The results are displayed in Table 10.1 (See p. 160). A total of 22 country cases were identified where aid restrictions were either imposed or threatened.[39] Four types of restrictive measures have been distinguished: full suspension; new project aid suspended; programme aid (or balance-of-payments support) suspended, overall reduction of aid allocation or disbursements on political grounds. In addition, a fifth catch-all category of 'other related measures' includes, for example, political statements or threats to take restrictive action, as well as non-aid measures (for example, arms embargoes).

Decision-making powers and institutional competencies regarding restrictive measures generally lie with intergovernmental mechanisms: the Council of Ministers (General Affairs) and the Common Foreign and Security Policy (CFSP) process. The Commission, however, is able to exert considerable discretionary power over measures other than full suspension. The jurisdiction of the European Parliament is limited to its veto power on budgetary matters, enabling it to block the signing of new agreements with non-ACP countries.[40]

Of the 22 country cases, the majority involve either full or partial suspension, split almost equally. Development co-operation was fully suspended in eight cases at some point during the time-period under study: Burundi, Liberia, Nigeria, Rwanda, Somalia, Sudan, Haiti and Turkey.[41] This involved withdrawal of all financial and technical assistance, except humanitarian aid. In two such cases, Liberia and Somalia, total suspension occurred *de facto*, rather than through formal decision-making processes, due to civil war and the collapse of national government. In another nine cases, new project aid was suspended, whilst current projects remained unaffected. Such partial measures were taken in The Gambia, Malawi, Niger, Togo, Zaire, China, Guatemala, Peru and Syria.[42] Means other than official suspension to reduce aid on political grounds are evident in two cases.[43] In Kenya and Equatorial Guinea the Commission has employed administrative means to slow down disbursements, for example, deferral of signatures. In three further countries, Lesotho, Sierra Leone and El Salvador, EU political statements threatened repercussions to their aid programmes if certain conditions were not met, with no further action deemed necessary.

In all cases restrictive action was taken either by the Council of Ministers or by the Commission, with the exceptions of Syria and Turkey. In the latter cases, the European Parliament has been responsible for sanctions through its refusal to give assent to new agreements. No initiative has been taken to restrict aid in the Mediterranean region by either the Commission or the Council.

Fair and equal treatment?

As stated in the introduction, a number of commentators on political conditionality have expressed doubts about the likelihood of consistent application.[44] What is the evidence after more than half a decade of policy implementation by the EU? Are judgements made in accordance with objective criteria about whom to impose restrictive measures against? Or has inconsistency prevailed?

In the following extended section, consistency of application is examined along three different lines of investigation: first, the regional distribution of country cases; second, the level of measures taken in relation to the degree of human rights abuses; and third, an inquiry into cases where no sanctions have been imposed despite evidence of gross violations of human rights, resulting in five further country studies.

Regional Distribution

Sub-Saharan Africa	Asia	Latin America and Caribbean	Middle East
15	1	4	2

What stands out from this regional breakdown is the overwhelming extent to which aid sanctions have been taken in sub-Saharan Africa, in 15 out of 22 country cases, in marked contrast to other regions. The non-democratic practices and human rights abuses of authoritarian regimes in other developing regions, particularly in Asia, North Africa and the Middle East, would appear to be subject to less scrutiny. Why is this and why has sub-Saharan Africa been selected for attention in this way?

Three reasons can account for this finding, one more defensible, the others much less so. First, political conditionality policies have arisen in the post-war context of the global emphasis on democratisation. Yet, it was particularly in sub-Saharan Africa in the first half of the 1990s that movements for democracy challenged the one-party states and military regimes throughout the continent, opening up situations where external leverage could be exerted in an attempt to influence the outcome in favour of the reformers. Second, as countries in sub-Saharan Africa are amongst the poorest and the most aid dependent in the world, it is here that donors are likely to regard aid sanctions as being most effective. Third, EU member states generally have the least to lose in sub-Saharan Africa by applying sanctions, with fewer countervailing pressures either in terms of economic interests (for example, trade and investment), or in geo-strategic interests, which have faded since the end of the Cold War.

Thus, the evidence indicates the large extent to which political conditionality has been applied against the poorest countries, particularly in Africa, in contrast to other countries with authoritarian polities, yet more rapidly growing economies. This confirms the suspicions of sceptics of political aid policies, that economic self-interest would prevail in relations with the latter group of countries.

Level of Sanctions

A variety of measures have been taken, not surprisingly given the differences in circumstances that arise. The relative 'toughness' of measures can be distinguished on the Commission's own rising scale, and by the

duration of their imposition. A total freeze on aid until there is improvement in human rights and conditions for democracy is evidently a more
vigorous measure than partial, short-term measures, although the latter,
or even mere threats, may be all that is required to achieve the desired
reform – but such cases are a minority. How have the levels of sanctions
been selected and what criteria have determined their relative robust-
ness? Is it the degree of infringements of human rights and democratic
processes? Or is the relative strength and weakness more related to the
presence of extraneous, countervailing factors?

There would appear to be little correlation between the level of sanctions imposed and the degree of human rights violations. There is evidence, however, of less robust measures being taken in countries where
the EU has greater economic and political interests. Three examples are
given of relatively weak sanctions taken in response to gross human
rights abuses and democratic reversals, accounted for by the prevalence
of self-interests.

China

In China after the Tiananmen Square massacre of June 1989, EU member states, in common with other Western nations, imposed aid and
trade sanctions, as well as suspending diplomatic relations.

New project aid was suspended and arms sales were banned. The aid
restrictions were maintained for a short duration, however, and relaxed
after only 16 months. 'Normalization' and then 'a gradual acceleration'
of development assistance soon followed. Yet no improvement in the
political situation had occurred. On the contrary, the 'relentless repression' of pro-democracy activists not only continued throughout 1990
and 1991,[45] but there was no ease-off by the mid-1990s, with reports of
'no fundamental change in the government's human rights policy',[46]
and that in fact 'in 1995 the authorities stepped up repression of
dissent'.[47] Aid sanctions against China can be seen as no more than a
token gesture, implemented in order to be seen to be taking some
action to appease domestic constituencies. The trade and investment
opportunities sought by EU member states in the rapidly expanding
Chinese economy required the expeditious abandonment of human
rights policies and the speedy resumption of 'business as usual'. Also, it
must not be forgotten that the accruement of export earnings is one
means through which the Chinese government maintains its grip on
power.

Nigeria

Nigeria would appear to be a clear-cut case for total aid suspension on human rights and democracy grounds. The protracted military-led transition to democracy was aborted at the final stage with the annulment of the presidential elections in June 1993. The formal return to military rule followed in November 1993 when General Abacha declared himself head of a new military government, dissolving the National Assembly and other regional and local democratic structures, and banning political parties and political activities. Subsequent events confirmed not only the anti-democratic but also the brutal nature of the military regime, with repression of the pro-democratic opposition and labour activists and with the detention of senior political figures, most notably the acknowledged winner of the presidential election, Moshood Abiola, and the former head of state, Olusegun Obasanjo.

Restrictions on aid as well as diplomatic and military sanctions were taken by the EU from July 1993, but for over two years could only be described as partial. It was not until November 1995, following the international outrage over the execution of Ken Saro-Wiwa and eight other Ogoni environmental activists, that a total freeze on development co-operation and the toughening-up of other measures, was adopted as a 'common position' by the Council of Ministers, legally binding on both multilateral and bilateral aid.[48] (See Table 10.1.) From July 1993 aid restrictions involved a review of all new projects, with approval only for those that assisted the poor. Existing projects were unaffected. Other related measures were suspension of military co-operation, visa restrictions for military personnel, and arms exports subject to a case-by-case review with 'the presumption of denial'. Member states were merely 'honour bound' to implement these measures, until their upgrading in November 1995.

The partial nature of measures taken for over two years sent a mixed message to the Nigerian military authorities, indicating a degree of concern and opposition to the turn of events, but not the unequivocal condemnation and tough punitive action one might have anticipated. The ambiguous and compromised nature of the EU's stance to the Nigerian military regime was most evident from the continued export of arms by some member states. The UK government was amongst those most culpable, responsible for issuing 20 new licences for arms exports in 1994,[49] as well as a fulfilment of existing contracts.[50] The new licences entailed a discreditable circumvention and disregard of the EU guidelines in two ways: first, ignoring 'the presumption of denial'; second, the sale of

so-called 'non-lethal' arms, and the phoney distinction of allowing arms
exports to the police but not the military, for example, CS gas and rubber
bullets.[51] Such equipment is obviously sought by the Nigerian authorities
for their continued 'ruthless suppression of dissent', as described by the US
Department of State.[52] Indeed, the UK government bears considerable
responsibility for the generally muted EU response to events in Nigeria
from mid-1993 to late 1995, being influential within CFSP discussions as
the former colonial power with considerable long-standing economic interests.

Tougher measures were introduced in November 1995, yet the EU
continued to eschew harder-hitting sanctions, for example, an oil embar-
go and the freezing of military bank accounts held in member states. It is
reported that the British and Dutch governments vetoed such measures,
doubtless with the interests in mind of Shell, the Anglo-Dutch oil multinational.[53]

Why were more vigorous aid sanctions not imposed earlier? Nigeria is
one of the very few sub-Saharan African countries where EU member
states have significant economic interests, in particular the oil extraction
activities of Shell. Britain especially has extensive commercial interests,
with exports of £480 million in 1994 and investments worth over £500
million.[54]

The Nigerian military regime benefits from and maintains its power
through its access to substantial oil revenues. In such a context, aid sanctions have to be combined with trade restrictions if effective leverage is
to be achieved. Yet, the serious intent of the EU in promoting democracy and human rights in Nigeria is questioned by its lack of preparedness
to impose measures that conflict with its own trade interests. In particular the UK government's resolve not to disrupt the profitability of oil
multinationals or of British arms manufacturers and traders has had a
corrosive effect on avowed policies.

Turkey

European Community aid to Turkey was suspended from 1980 until late
1995, when the European Parliament gave its consent to a customs
union, paving the way for new aid and trade deals. Suspension originally
followed the military coup in 1980 and the subsequent systematic violation of human rights, including the crushing of trade unions and leftist
groups. This contrasted with US policy, with Turkey for many years the
third largest recipient of US foreign assistance, surpassed by Israel and
Egypt only. Yet, in the 1990s, the continued suspension of assistance to

Turkey has been due to the European Parliament, who have opposed on human rights grounds the efforts by the Council of Ministers and the Commission to re-establish aid and trade co-operation. Parliament's concern in particular has been the repression of the Kurdish minority in Turkey and the violation of international humanitarian law by the Turkish army in their actions against the guerrillas of the separatist Kurdish Workers' Party (the PKK), in which Kurdish villages have been evacuated, bombed and destroyed in operations described as 'savage'.[55] Whilst condemning both the terrorist activities of the PKK and the abusive counterinsurgency campaign of the Turkish authorities, the European Parliament urged the Turkish government to seek a resolution with democratic Kurds, recognising their right to autonomy and to use their own language.[56] In contrast, at a time when the human rights situation was described as 'worsening significantly' by the US Assistant Secretary of State, John Shattack,[57] the EU was negotiating a customs union with the Turkish government. This was signed in March 1995 and is one of the closest links aside from full membership. The required ratification of this treaty by the European Parliament was initially refused in April 1995, with future support made conditional on improvements in the Turkish government's human rights record. Some legal reforms followed, notably amendments to the 1991 Anti-Terror Law, and, under considerable pressure from the Council and the Commission,[58] Parliament ratified the treaty in late 1995.

EU inter-governmental wishes to re-establish close links with the Turkish authorities, including an aid and trade package, appear to be influenced by Turkey's strategic position and the desire not to disrupt the NATO military alliance, with human rights issues pushed aside. As a lower middle-income state, Turkey is not aid dependent, and aid restrictions will have limited economic impact. Nevertheless, given the strong desire of most recent Turkish governments to join the EU, such sanctions do convey a powerful symbolic message, with the potential to leverage improvements in the human rights situation, notably the treatment of the Kurds. Any such potential was lost, however, by the lack of a coherent and consistent human rights policy, with European Parliament conditionality undermined by the other EU institutions.

In sum, the general lack of correlation between the degree of human rights abuses and the level of sanctions imposed indicate a failure to implement human rights policy on the basis of objective, non-selective criteria. The three country cases demonstrate in particular that the level of response is muted and ambiguous where EU members' economic and political interests are more manifest. In the case of China, the strong rhetorical condemnation of the Tiananmen Square massacre was not translated into punitive measures that were any more than a token appeasement of domestic constituencies, as the industrialized nations rapidly resumed competition for strongholds in the expanding Chinese market. The EU has demonstrated a preparedness to impose aid sanctions in sub-Saharan Africa more than in any other region. Yet in Nigeria, one of very few African states where EU members have significant commercial interests, the military authorities were able to display a contemptuous disregard for human rights and democracy for over two years, while continuing to receive arms exports, before a more robust set of measures was adopted as a 'common position'. In Turkey, inter-governmental resolve to strengthen ties, primarily for strategic and security reasons, has overpowered any human rights concerns, whilst simultaneously undermining Parliamentary action and disregarding a real opportunity to leverage improvements in a deteriorating human rights situation.

No sanctions

The pattern of inconsistent application of policy is given further emphasis by an inquiry into a number of countries where no restrictions on aid have been imposed by the EU, despite government records of gross and persistent human rights violations. Five mini country case-studies are presented here, notably all in regions other than sub-Saharan Africa. Each of these examines the human rights and democracy situation, provides a brief profile of EU aid, and analyses why punitive measures have not been taken.[59]

Indonesia

The example of Indonesia provides some of the most compelling evidence of the inconsistency and double standards of Northern governments in their non-implementation of human rights and democracy policies. Two human rights issues remain prominent. First, there is the indisputable evidence of continuing 'serious human rights abuses' committed by the government in the context of a 'strongly authoritarian' political system with 'severe limitations on freedoms of speech, press, assembly, and association', as described by the US Department of State.[60] Similarly, Human Rights Watch perceives a pattern of abuse 'characterized by military intervention in virtually all aspects of public life and by the arbitrary exercise of authority by President Suharto'.[61] The armed forces have sizeable representation in the legislature, allocated 100 (out of 500) seats, appointed directly by the President. Specific mechanisms of political control include the banning of political parties, with the Communist Party remaining outlawed since 1965; press censorship, with three publications closed in June 1994 in a clampdown prior to the APEC Summit in November in Jakarta; the denial of workers' rights, notably the ability to form independent trade unions; and the violent dispersal of peaceful demonstrations.[62]

Second, there is the continuing occupation of East Timor, invaded and annexed in 1975, in which between one-fifth to one-third of the indigenous population is estimated to have been killed.[63] The Santa Cruz massacre in November 1991 re-focused world attention on East Timor, with smuggled film showing an estimated 200 unarmed mourners killed by the Indonesian army at the funeral of a young independence supporter.

On human rights grounds, the Indonesian government is a clear candidate for the application of aid sanctions, as a means of pressurising the government to implement quite specific reforms, for example the protection of workers' rights or press freedom, as well as to enter UN-brokered negotiations to resolve the status of East Timor. Yet, with the exception of the Dutch in late 1991, no aid restrictions have been imposed on Indonesia by the European Community or its member states. EU assistance itself, as part of its agreement with the ASEAN members, amounts to between $12 and 15 million (net) each year. As stated above, EU–ASEAN co-operation contains no human rights provisions, and, though formally expired, is maintained on the basis of the old agreement. Amongst EU member states, Germany and France are major donors to Indonesia, whilst it was ranked the third highest recipient of British aid in 1995/6.

How do we explain the absence of aid conditionality in this case? Trading interests evidently take priority. Indonesia's sustained economic growth, combined with its large population, makes it an attractive market, as well as a prominent location of foreign direct investment, with the latter reaching record levels in 1995. Western European governments, themselves influenced by powerful business interests, wish to use development aid to improve their own 'market position' within Indonesia, and to enhance the financial opportunities available. More specifically as regards East Timor, Indonesia's own economic interests in its mineral riches are shared by the industrialised nations. In 1991, the Indonesian and the Australian governments signed a contract with 12 companies to extract a billion barrels of oil from Timorese waters, the consortium being led by Royal Dutch Shell (joint British and Dutch) and Chevron (US).[64]

In such a context, any human rights concerns are subordinated to those of trade and swiftly overwhelmed.

Sri Lanka

Despite having a multi-party democratic polity, Sri Lankan politics and society have been dominated since the 1980s by armed conflict on two fronts. First, Tamil secessionists, the Liberation Tigers of Tamil Eelam (LTTE), have fought with government forces since 1983 for a separate state in the north-east of the island, with almost 20 000 killed. Second, in the south, Marxist opposition led by the *Janatha Vimukthi Peramuna* (JVP), the People's Liberation Front, engaged in an armed insurgency against the government, most intense between 1987 and 1990, with a further five-figure death toll before their defeat by the security forces.[65] Undoubtedly gross human rights violations have been committed by all sides, including civilian massacres, with ample evidence documented by international human rights organisations. Guerrilla groups, however, do not receive official development aid, and the concern here is that government atrocities have not been the subject of any EU reprimands or sanctions. Government forces were responsible for detentions, 'disappearances' and extrajudicial executions on a massive scale in both the north-east and the south.[66] A trend in decreased human rights abuses from 1992 was reversed with the abandonment by the LTTE in April 1995 of a brief ceasefire and the resumption of fighting. Human rights abuses by both sides in the renewed conflict have included hundreds of civilian deaths in government air bombings.[67]

Germany, the Netherlands, and the UK are significant aid donors to the Sri Lankan government; EU aid has been relatively small, on average about $8 million (net) between 1990 and 1994. A new trade and co-operation agreement, however, between the EU and the Sri Lankan government came into effect in April 1995 and included a human rights and democracy clause as an essential element. The upsurge of human rights abuses since then, including by government forces, has not led so far to the invoking of that clause by the EU.

Why has there been no linkage of aid to improvements in the Sri Lankan government's human rights record, either at the height of the civil conflicts in the late 1980s and early 1990s or since mid-1995? Three reasons are explored.

First, an up-turn in the human rights picture in Sri Lanka is discernible from 1991 onwards, and the lack of donor conditionality could be attributed to this progressive trend. Such an explanation is inadequate, however. Continued aid could have been linked to specific human rights improvements, for example, the investigation of extrajudicial killings and disappearances linked to the security forces and the prosecution of those responsible. Such conditionality measures would have been particularly appropriate, given that human rights reforms were being undertaken not by a new government but by the old regime, itself responsible for the past abuses. This opportunity was not taken by the donors.

Second, any inclination to criticise the Sri Lankan government's appalling human rights record was probably countered by an ideological sympathy towards the regime, given its formal democratic credentials and the violent opposition it faced from both separatist and Marxist guerrillas. This could account for, though not justify, the disposition to turn a 'blind eye' to the abusive counterinsurgency methods used by government forces.

Third, trade is also a significant determinant, and it would appear that trading relations with Sri Lanka have generally been accorded a greater priority than human rights. During the 1980s, the Sri Lankan government introduced economic liberalisation policies, offering new prospects for direct foreign investment, especially in 'export-processing zones'. Consequentially, trade has grown in importance with many EU members. The new 'trade and co-operation' agreement signed between the EU and the Sri Lankan government in 1995 specifically emphasised 'substantial development and diversification of trade' in the context of rapidly expanding trade relations, with EU exports to Sri Lanka having increased by 41 per cent between 1993 and 1994, and Sri Lanka's exports by 20 per cent.[68]

Algeria

Since the cancellation of the parliamentary elections in January 1992, with the opposition Islamic Salvation Front (FIS) clear front-runners, Algeria has degenerated into a bloody civil war between the military-led government and radical Islamic armed groups, with unofficial estimates of up to 50 000 Algerians killed by late 1995, including many unarmed civilians. Gross human rights violations have been committed by both sides. The Islamist extremists, notably the *Groupe Islamique Armée* (GIA – Armed Islamic Group), are waging a campaign of terror and intimidation, responsible for countless atrocities since January 1992. For its part the government has engaged in torture, 'disappearances' and arbitrary killings against both the armed Islamist groups and unarmed civilians.[69] The abuse of women is a highly disturbing aspect of the war; women being subject to attacks by both sides.

Algeria is an undeniable example of where an abrupt halt to the democratization process through military intervention, with subsequent gross human rights violations by state forces, has not entailed aid sanctions. On the contrary, development assistance from the European Commission has increased dramatically, from approximately $10m. in the early 1990s to $46m. and $37m. in 1993 and 1994 respectively. Aid from France, the biggest donor, has also increased, with grants of over $100m. each year since 1991. This provides a sharp contrast to the punitive measures taken against other countries where a breakdown in democratisation has occurred, notably in sub-Saharan Africa.[70] Why were such measures not taken in the case of Algeria? Why have different standards of human rights and democratic practices apparently been applied?

Within the EU, the French government is the key player, providing unconditional support to the military-led Algerian government in their attempts to crush the radical Islamist opposition. Condemnation of terrorist violence is not matched by the French condemnation of that by Algerian state forces. This lack of evenhandedness has not been publicly contested by any other member state. EU policy is driven by the strong motivation to stem the rise of Islamic fundamentalism. Radical Islam is seen as a threat to political stability in the region, and an Islamist victory in Algeria is feared as leading to a domino effect in neighbouring countries and a wave of migration to southern Europe. As in the struggle to defeat communism before it, there are no objections to the means used, including violations of human rights and the basic tenets of humanitarian law. In the conflict between principles and self-interests, the latter win handsomely. The priority is the defeat of an ideological opponent in Europe's 'backyard'.

Algeria may be an exception, but it is an example of the recurrence of selectivity in applying human rights criteria. Selectivity was pervasive during the Cold War, and ideology was the key factor behind condemning human rights abuses by some governments, whilst condoning the abuses by others.

Egypt

The constitution of the republic of Egypt describes it as a multi-party democracy in which human rights are guaranteed. Egyptian politics and society have long been characterised, however, by the suppression of internal dissent by the government, involving restrictions on democratic processes and abuses of civil and political rights. The primary mechanism is the state of emergency in force without interruption since October 1981, with broad powers of detention resulting in tens of thousands of arbitrary arrests of 'political suspects' without charge or trial, and related torture.[71] The most recent elections in 1995 were characterised by the jailing of leading opposition candidates and campaigners.[72] Such undemocratic practices have resulted in a political system so dominated by the ruling National Democratic Party that the US Department of State, hardly an antagonist of the Egyptian government, recognises that 'the people do not have a meaningful ability to change their government'.[73]

Moreover, the overall human rights situation has deteriorated considerably with the escalation from 1992 of armed opposition to the Egyptian government from radical Islamist groups, with both sides culpable of serious abuses. The response of the Egyptian government to the armed opposition has been two-fold. The first is the intensification of pre-existing practices of violent repression. Such methods are primarily directed against the Islamist militants, but with 'frequent victimization of non-combatants as well'.[74] Allegations of extrajudicial killings by the security forces have become common in an environment of impunity.[75] The second response has been to generalise the state clampdown, with significant restrictions on the civil and political liberties of non-violent opponents and other dissenting voices, including the curtailment of press freedoms.

Egypt receives very substantial ODA, with gross bilateral assistance of between $2.5 billion and almost $4 billion each year between 1990 and 1994. The US is by far the biggest donor, contributing over $2 billion per annum in foreign aid, though the majority of this is not ODA but military assistance. However, European donors also contribute very sizeable amounts of ODA, notably France, Germany, Italy and The Netherlands. German and French ODA, including debt write-offs, has averaged $424m. and $265m. respectively per annum between 1990 and 1994. The EU itself also provides very considerable assistance, with net average disbursements of $121.8 m. per annum in the same period, making this lower middle-income country one of the largest recipients of Community aid.

The failure to link economic aid to human rights and democracy conditions replicates features in common with Algeria, though with the US as the key player to whom the EU states tend to defer. Human rights abuses and undemocratic practices are again conspicuously ignored in the context of overriding foreign policy considerations.

Egypt occupies an important geo-strategic location in relation to the Middle East, North Africa and the Horn of Africa. A friendly government in Egypt fulfils a number of roles important to the achievement of EU foreign policy objectives. First, Egypt continues to be an essential ally for the success of the Arab–Israeli peace process. Second, a friendly Egypt plays a key role in mobilising the support of moderate Arab states as circumstances arise, most notably in the Gulf War of 1991 after the Iraqi invasion of Kuwait. Third, the retention of a pro-Western government in Egypt is a requisite for the aim of fostering a wider alliance of moderate forces that share the goals of free markets and secular, liberal states. Fourth, related to this last point, is the struggle against Islamic fundamentalism, seen as the foremost threat to EU objectives of future stability in the Middle East.

In reviewing the importance of an allied Egyptian government to EU foreign policy objectives, it becomes evident that the silence on human rights abuses and undemocratic practices is not merely due to such considerations taking priority. The repression of the opposition and the restrictions on democratic processes in themselves serve Western governments' interests in maintaining the ruling political elite in power. In contrast, an active, multi-party polity would raise the potential for undesired changes in the power-holders, particularly when the main opposition is the Muslim Brotherhood. It is a silence by the Western powers, both the US and the EU, which condones the actions of the Egyptian government as necessary for their own objectives.

Colombia

A democracy in name, Colombia is one of the most violent societies in the world, with approximately 30 000 Colombians murdered each year, including about 10 political killings each day. Colombia is best known for drug-trafficking-related violence, but the rate of political murders has been the highest in the Americas for almost the past decade, matched only by Peru at the height of the *Sendero Luminoso* insurgency. Political killings stem mainly from the armed conflict between leftist guerrilla groups and government security forces allied with paramilitary groups. The latter also target non-violent political parties and economic and social groups in death squad activities.

Human rights violations are committed by all sides. Yet it is the role of government security forces and the allied paramilitary groups that stands out, responsible for the majority of the 3000 to 4000 political murders each year.[76]

The impunity with which the armed forces and the paramilitary groups can operate is a principal cause of the continuing gross abuse of human rights in Colombia. A fundamental flaw in the Colombian judicial system is the jurisdiction of military tribunals over cases involving members of the armed forces, as well as over civilians on public order offences. In its 1996 Report, Human Rights Watch states how 'Military tribunals continued systematically to cover up crimes and absolve the military and police officers involved'.[77] The Colombian government has repeatedly failed to reform this judicial defect, and there has been no attempt by Northern governments to leverage such a change through aid conditionality. Indeed, there is no indication of any aid restrictions.

The biggest provider of foreign assistance is the US, though most of this is non-ODA. The largest ODA donor in recent years has been Germany. European Commission aid has risen in the first half of the 1990s from a modest $5.2m. (net) in 1990 to $12–14m. in 1993 and 1994. EU aid to the Colombian government is part of the agreement with Andean Pact countries, signed in 1993 with a human rights and democracy clause as an essential element. However, despite the overwhelming evidence of Colombian government forces' involvement in gross human rights abuses, no restrictive measures have been taken. Why has the Colombian government escaped criticism? Three reasons are put forward.

First, the EU is less disposed to impose conditionality on a democratically elected civilian government with a rhetorical commitment to human rights. Yet, the example of Colombia vividly demonstrates how formal democracy far from guarantees the protection of civil and political liberties. A government must be judged on its willingness and effectiveness to combat and prevent abuses, and the efforts of the Colombian government in this respect are woefully inadequate.

Second, there is deference by European governments to the US as the most influential external actor. US policy in Colombia is dominated by its 'war on drugs' in the Andean countries. This entails the provision of financial aid, equipment and training to the very police and military forces that are responsible for gross human rights abuses, making it difficult to square with human rights concerns.

A third factor is an ideological leftover from the Cold War. There remains a predilection towards support for governments engaged in 'counterinsurgency' activities to defeat leftist guerrillas and to play down the human rights abuses committed in doing so.

Summary of findings

The evidence from all three lines of investigation reveal a pattern of selective and inconsistent application of policy. First, the regional analysis of the 22 country cases displayed the overwhelming extent to which aid sanctions have been taken in sub-Saharan Africa, where EU members have little to lose. In comparison, restrictive measures are much less common in other regions where countervailing interests are more prevalent.

Second, the general lack of correlation between the degree of human rights violations and the level of sanctions imposed indicates a failure to implement human rights policy on the basis of objective criteria. This is illustrated in particular by the evidence from the three country cases, China, Nigeria and Turkey, all demonstrating how the level of response to human rights abuses is muted and ambiguous where EU members' economic and political interests are more manifest.

Third, the evidence of the five 'non-cases', where aid sanctions are conspicuous by their absence, provides further confirmation of the subordination of human rights and democracy policies to other dominant foreign policy concerns. In the Cold War period this was mainly attributable to geo-strategic considerations. These remain evident, especially in the Middle East, where the retention of friendly governments in order to maintain Western European influence takes priority over human rights issues. Post-Cold War, however, other factors carry more weight. Foremost of these is the pursuit of economic self-interest by EU member states, with trade and investment as the primary countervailing factor, indicated in particular by policy in East Asia. In addition, old and new elements of ideology continue to result in selective condemnations. In continuity with Cold War practices, human rights violations by governments engaged in civil wars against left-wing guerrillas tend to be overlooked, as the examples of Colombia and Sri Lanka show. New Western fears concerning the rise of Islamic Fundamentalism in Algeria and Egypt have led to fresh examples of government abuses of human rights in counterinsurgency campaigns being tolerated and condoned.

Whilst not ignoring the complexities of all four civil war situations and the difficulties encountered by governments faced by insurgent groups, it remains paramount that objective judgements on alleged human rights abuses must be based on the nature of the acts perpetrated and not by whom. Failure to conduct counterinsurgency within the framework of international humanitarian law and with full respect for human rights should be condemned. These four cases of civil wars also indicate a tendency to overlook the roots of violent opposition in the undemocratic practices of incumbent regimes, for example in Algeria and Egypt, and a failure to condition development assistance on specific political reforms, for example the flawed justice system in Colombia.

CONCLUSION

A normative agenda and the significance of consistency

This chapter has investigated the implementation of political conditionality against a normative background of the fair and equal treatment of all nations. It has examined two policy instruments, human rights and democracy clauses and aid sanctions, and assessed their application on the criterion of consistency.

The enquiry into the insertion of **human rights and democracy clauses** in development co-operation agreements revealed a lack of consistency, up to the present. Whilst recognising the Commission's attempts to establish a standard formula, current patterns of its inclusion remain characterised by inconsistency within and particularly between regions. The primacy of the EU's economic interests over human rights in regions of economic expansion is shown in particular by the lack of insistence in re-negotiating the expired agreement with ASEAN to include a human rights and democracy clause. Similarly the priority accorded by the EU to external relations with countries on its southern Mediterranean borders, as indicated by the declaration of the Euro–Mediterranean Partnership, is clearly motivated by trade and security objectives. There is a stated intention to insert a human rights and democracy clause in the new Association Agreements currently being negotiated. It would appear likely, however, that the EU will seek to square the human rights circle in order not to jeopardise new agreements with some governments who are currently gross violators of human rights and democratic principles.[78]

The enquiry into **aid sanctions**, recently concluded, was conducted along three lines of investigation, all demonstrating a pattern of selective and inconsistent application of policy, with frequent subordination of human rights and democracy policies to other predominant concerns.

Those unsympathetic to my line of argument could point out that these findings are not only unsurprising but also could be anticipated, given that the promotion of human rights and democracy is only one of a number of foreign policy issues that impact on development co-operation. Questions such as the following could be posited. How can political conditionality be considered separately from other foreign policy goals? Is it not naive to expect that EU member states will place human rights and democracy at the centre of their common foreign policy, or that such concerns will take precedence over issues of trade or perceived 'security'? Rather, is it not to be expected that EU positions will be adopted on a country-by-country basis precisely through examination of the range of foreign policy issues, with human rights concerns often competing unequally with other more compelling interests? This may lead to inconsistency when decisions on aid sanctions are examined in terms of one criterion only, that of human rights, but is this not an inevitable aspect of policy implementation in the real world?

On the other hand, are such pragmatic or realist arguments themselves satisfactory? There are counter-arguments. Two points follow. First, it is obviously correct that human rights concerns co-exist with, and cannot be addressed in isolation from other foreign policy objectives. Yet the evidence presented here demonstrates that when *any* other foreign policy goal comes into conflict with the promotion of human rights and democracy, then it is the latter that is abandoned. In a hierarchy of foreign policy objectives, an element of consistency is that human rights and democracy concerns are at the bottom of the pile.

Second, it is itself inappropriate to examine policy implementation in this area solely from a realist or pragmatic perspective. There *is* a normative dimension to this policy agenda which the EU has *itself* introduced. The post-Cold War emphasis on respect for human rights and democratic principles is to raise both foreign policy and development policy on to a moral plane, based on a set of norms that are regarded as universal. By making such norms a condition of development assistance, and by including them in a development contract, they must be binding on all parties. This requires both donors and recipients to act according to defined standards. If EU members, having stipulated the norms themselves, then act more in accordance with self-interests, this not only exposes them to the accusation of double standards but also undermines the credibility and legitimacy of the whole policy agenda. If donors' commitment to the principles of human rights and democracy is at best partial and dependent on the lack of competing self-interests, they can hardly require development partners to abide by those principles in a manner that commands respect.

Towards fair and equal treatment: some recommendations

The aim of this chapter is critically to evaluate current donor practice in this area and to seek a common normative framework, both acceptable to all parties, South and North, and within which the participation and authorship of recipient nations is enhanced. As a contribution to such discussions, the following recommendations are put forward, endeavouring primarily to internationalise policy implementation.

Definition of concepts

Human rights and democracy are concepts which easily roll off the tongue, and to which few dare to voice their opposition. Yet, notwithstanding this overall consensus, it is necessary to define the concepts precisely. But, more than five years after the initial Council Resolution of November 1991, the EU has yet to provide such definitions, despite the introduction of a human rights and democratic principles clause as an essential element of development co-operation agreements.

As a threshold requirement, **it is recommended that human rights refer to civil and political rights only, as defined in the UN International Covenant on Civil and Political Rights**. The ICCPR has been ratified by the majority of the world's nation states, both industrialised and developing, as well as re-affirmed in the African and American regional conventions. This does not contradict the 'indivisibility' of human rights. In contrast to the 'aspirational' nature of economic, social and cultural rights, civil and political rights are wholly appropriate as a threshold condition: they are subject to implementation without delay or deferment, whatsoever the level of economic development of a ratifying state.

Defining democracy remains a contested and contentious subject, with disputes in particular between procedural and substantive variants. This author is an advocate of the latter type, but nevertheless recommends that the **democratic principles clause focuses on procedural elements, referring specifically to regular, free and fair elections, as well as the pre-requisite of civil and political rights**. (A more substantive definition is appropriate for positive programmes to support democratisation.)

Assessment criteria and performance indicators

Having achieved definitional clarity, it is then possible to develop **an inventory of criteria by which country performance will be assessed, and of measurable performance indicators**. Again, five years into this policy agenda, these tasks remain to be achieved.

Transparency

In carrying out the above tasks, it is essential that the process is characterised both by agreement between parties and by transparency. As the allocation of development assistance is now linked to political principles, it is necessary that recipient governments are both involved in dialogue about and fully aware of the conditions being laid down. Transparency is also required regarding which violations will trigger which restrictive measures in response.

Monitoring performance

At present, monitoring and evaluation of country performance appear to occur on a fairly *ad hoc* basis, mainly responding to crisis situations as they arise.

Within the EU there are three institutional mechanisms with poten- tial input into such processes: the Commission Human Rights and Democracy Unit (DGI); the Parliament Human Rights Sub-Committee; and the CFSP mechanisms, linked to the Council of Ministers, which in- clude a Human Rights Working Group and regional working groups. However, there are constraints of both capacity and jurisdiction which limit the input of all these bodies.[79]

Thus, there is a need to allocate the responsibility of monitoring coun- try performances to a specific institution and to ensure that it is carried out satisfactorily and objectively. To the latter end, **the use of pre-exist- ing monitoring mechanisms** is recommended, particularly those of the **UN system of human rights**.[80] There are both pragmatic and normative benefits to greater use of UN monitoring bodies. They are well estab- lished, with experience both of standard setting and measuring compli- ance, and encompass both sets of rights. They are endowed with legitimacy, mutually acceptable to all parties, and can contribute to the development of a 'commonly shared normative framework'.[81]

Internationalisation

A common normative framework could be enhanced further by interna- tionalisation of responsibility for carrying out the above tasks. They could be **delegated to a non-EU body, for example, an existing UN agen- cy**.[82] As well as the initial one-off tasks of defining concepts and criteria, the responsibilities of such a body could include both ongoing country performance monitoring and the investigation of instances of perceived violations as they arise. This international body would have the compe- tence to make recommendations, although the appropriate decision- making body would have the discretion to accept or disregard its advice.

Decision-making

The EU prefers to discuss human rights and democracy clauses not in the language of conditionality but in terms of a joint commitment between two equal partners to universal principles, based on dialogue and consensus.[83] However, the reality of decision-making regarding aid sanctions is of unilateral actions by the EU, notwithstanding the consultative mechanisms of the Bulgarian clause and the revised Lomé Convention. Powers remain concentrated in the hands of the Council of Ministers and the Commission.[84] A recommendation is that **decision-making powers be relinquished to joint bodies**, organised on a regional basis. These could be based on the 'Association Councils' within co-operation agreements. Developing country governments should have a majority of members.

Concluding Remarks

The EU has chosen to move its foreign policy, and hence its development policy, to an arena where it is appealing to certain norms as universally binding – that is, respect for human rights and democratic principles. The implications are that inconsistency in policy implementation cannot easily be dismissed as a function of conflicting foreign policy objectives. The universal nature of these principles itself requires that their application be objective and non-selective. The recommendations above are put forward in the spirit of forging policy instruments in which the values involved are shared and with ownership not restricted to Northern donor governments. The intention is that the principles of human rights and democracy inform and permeate policy practice at all levels. Having introduced the normative dimension, it is imperative that the EU adheres to the principles it has espoused. The alternative is a rhetorical commitment only and a practice that continues to be based on self-interest and characterised by an assertion of power over the poorest and weakest nations.

Table 10.1 EU aid sanctions January 1990–January 1996

Country	Aid reductions (on political grounds)	Programme aid suspended	New project aid suspended	Full suspension of aid	Other related measures
BURUNDI				De facto suspension from October 1993 to October 1994 of development aid due to political instability. (Large amounts of humanitarian aid.) Willingness to provide longer-term aid to support reconstruction efforts stated in October 1994, after special donor conference in September. An EU 'common position' was adopted in March 1995, which re-stated such commitments, including assistance to reconstruct democracy and the rule of law. However, disbursements have been adversely affected by a perceived lack of both representative government and efforts to end the violence. Aid suspended again in April 1996, upheld following the military coup in July 1996.	
EQUATOR-IAL GUINEA	Not officially suspend-ed, but described as 'put on ice' in 1994 owing to repeated human rights violations and repres-sion of opposition parties (European Commission, 1996).				

KENYA	Allocation of ECU 140m. under EDF7 (1991–5). By the end of 1994, only 20 per cent had been committed and less than 5 per cent disbursed due mainly to economic and administrative reasons, but with a political dimension involved.	Since 1990 to date.	new projects reviewed on a case-by-case basis, with approval only for those that help needy people. This partial suspension followed the military coup and the lack of progress towards the restoration of democracy.
LESOTHO			Threats to suspend aid were made twice in 1994. The first in February after rumblings of military action against the newly elected government, with warnings of 'serious consequences' for the development co-operation programme. Further statement after the August coup, warning that relations would be

Table 10.1 *(contd.)*

Country	Aid reductions (on political grounds)	Programme aid suspended	New project aid suspended	Full suspension of aid	Other related measures
					'reviewed', including the development co-operation programme, unless democracy restored.
LIBERIA				De facto suspension of development co-operation since 1990 to date. Large amounts of humanitarian assistance.	
MALAWI			Partial freeze from May 1992 to November 1993, in line with decision taken at Consultative Group meeting. Suspension lifted after agreement by government to hold elections.		
NIGER			Following the military coup, development co-operation suspended from 29 January 1996 for an initial period of six months, except for aid directly benefiting the poor. This action was invoked in relation to Article 366a of the revised Lomé IV Convention, signed in November 1995. A progressive restoration of co-operation was		

	announced on 28 June 1996, following a constitutional referendum and the lifting of the state of emergency. However, the presidential elections held in July 1996 were condemned as not free and fair, with aid restrictions again under discussion.	From November 1995 a freeze on bilateral and multilateral co-operation, following the executions of the Ogoni 9. A 'common position' was adopted by the EU Council of Ministers on 20 November 1995, including a total suspension of co-operation, with the exception of projects promoting human rights, democratization and poverty alleviation through local, non-governmental channels. The Head of the EU Delegation in Nigeria was recalled in December 1995.	The following announced to be implemented by member states: (1) 14 July 1993: (a) Suspension of military co-operation; (b) Visa restrictions on members of the military and security forces. (2) December 1993: Arms exports subject to review on a case-by-case basis 'with a presumption of denial'; exemptions of non-lethal equipment. (3) 20 November 1995: (a) Total embargo on arms sales;
NIGERIA	From July 1993, all new projects reviewed on a case-by-case basis. Guidelines agreed in September 1994 stating that only projects that assist the poor and not the government to be approved. From January 1995 all new projects suspended due to administrative difficulties (e.g. an unrealistic exchange rate) as well as the political dimension.		

Table 10.1 (contd.)

Country	Aid reductions (on political grounds)	Programme aid suspended	New project aid suspended	Full suspension of aid	Other related measures
					(b) visa restrictions broadened to government members.
					4) 4 December 1995: (a) expulsion of military personnel in Nigerian diplomatic missions; (b) Sports sanctions by refusal of visas.
RWANDA				From April until 24 October 1994, when gradual re-establishment of development co-operation announced, assuming conditions of respect for human rights and progress towards national reconciliation were met (Courier No 149). However, restoration of development co-operation continued to be problematic, with EU refusing in November 1994 to release committed funds of $ 124 million unless the RPF-led government broadened its base (generally considered to be due to pressure from French government). Development aid again suspended in May 1995 following the massacres at the Kibeho refugee camp. Discussions on resump-	Rehabilitation assistance pledged by donors at Round Table in June 1996. No political conditionality attached, though pressure on government to restore the justice system, to improve human rights, and to facilitate the repatriation of refugees.

SIERRA LEONE				Statement expressing concern about the internal military coup in January 1996 and that the planned democratic transition should not be effected. Implied threat that continued support would be withdrawn if elections did not go ahead. Multi-party elections were held in March 1996, the first since 1967, with a return to civilian government.
SOMALIA (Somalia has not ratified Lomé IV, signed in 1989.)			De facto suspension from end of 1991 to date.	
SUDAN			From 1990 to date on human rights grounds. Discussions on the co-operation programme under Lomé IV were abandoned and no agreement made.	Stabex transfers frozen since 1991.
TOGO		From January 1992, following the breakdown of the democratization process, the dissolution of the provisional legislative assembly and the return to power of President		Political statement in November 1992 on the need for a return to constitutional rule, respect for human rights and the rule of law as 'necessary

Table 10.1   *(contd.)*

Country	Aid reductions (on political grounds)	Programme aid suspended	New project aid suspended	Full suspension of aid	Other related measures
			Eyadema in December 1991. Partial resumption announced in March 1995 (rural development, education, HIV/AIDS), 'to encourage Togo's efforts in the field of democratization' (CFSP Statement of 7 March 1995).		Conditions' for development co-operation
ZAIRE			From early 1992 to date after suspension of the National Conference and the failure of progress in democratization.		
BURMA (MYANMAR)				De facto as no agreement entered into.	
CHINA			From June 1989 to 23 October 1990, when restrictions on new projects relaxed. In February 1992, EU foreign ministers reaffirmed a progressive normalization of development assistance to China, with priorities being stated as good governance, poverty alleviation, minorities, economic		Ban on arms sales and military co-operation remained after October 1990 relaxation of aid measures.

CUBA No co-operation agreement, humanitarian aid and aid to NGOs only.	reform and the environment. Since then there has been a gradual acceleration of aid (European Commission 1994c, p. 15).		Initiation by EU in 1995 of political dialogue, with the aim of concluding a trade and economic co-operation agreement, regarded as the best means to strengthen a transition to a market economy and political pluralism. The process of drafting negotiating directives for an agreement was suspended in May 1996, however, citing lack of progress by the Cuban government on both political reforms and economic liberalization. Informal dialogue to continue.
EL SALVADOR Aid provided through a regional co-operation agreement with Central			Political statements: 1. March 1993 – expressing concern over Salvadorian government's unconditional amnesty for those implicated in human

Table 10.1 *(contd.)*

Country	Aid reductions (on political grounds)	Programme aid suspended	New project aid suspended	Full suspension of aid	Other related measures
American countries since 1985. This arises out of the San José Process, annual meetings between the EU and Central American leaders, seeking to resolve the regional conflict. The second co-operation agreement, signed in 1993, innovatively included support for (i) democratization and human rights; and (ii) refugees (De Feyter *et al.*, 1995, p. 29).					rights abuses during the war in contradiction to the recommendations of the UN Truth Commission report. 2. October 1993 – expressing concern about renewed political violence and murders, especially targeted against FMLN members. Also European Parliament resolution of 18 November 1993 reminding the Salvadorian authorities of the democratic clause in the new co-operation agreement.

GUATEMA-LA (See El Salvador)	On 28 May 1993, immediately following President Serranos' self-coup, dissolving Congress and the Supreme Court. He was forced to resign one week later.		
HAITI		From 3 October 1991 to 14 October 1994 development co-operation was suspended after the military coup against President Aristide's government. Aid restored after re-instatement of Aristide and lifting of UN sanctions. (Humanitarian and emergency aid maintained throughout.)	
PERU [Largest programme of assistance in Latin America in 1994 (European Commission, 1995c)]	New aid suspended from April 1992–March 1993, following President Fujimori's self-coup, dissolving Congress and suspending the judiciary.		Statement on 8 April 1992 calling on President Fujimori to restore democratic institutions as soon as possible. Relations restored gradually after new Congressional elections in November 1992, despite their boycott by the main political parties.

Table 10.1 (contd.)

Country	Aid reductions (on political grounds)	Programme aid suspended	New project aid suspended	Full suspension of aid	Other related measures
SYRIA	The European Parliament blocked a new 5-year package during 1992 and 1993, refusing to give its assent on a number of occasions on human rights grounds. Finally, at the end of 1993 the EP's assent was obtained for this fourth financial protocol (1992–6) with Mediterranean countries.		Sanctions were imposed from 1986 until October 1990, when restrictions were removed (*Financial Times*, 23 October 1990).		
TURKEY				Bilateral aid suspended since 1980 on human rights grounds. However, this was lifted in December 1995 with the European Parliament finally giving approval to the creation of a customs union between the EU and Turkey, on condition that the human rights record is monitored. As well as the trading advantages, this is a necessary step to eventual membership of the EU, and also releases £600 million in aid.	

Notes

1. ASEAN stands for the Association of South East Asian Nations, and its long-standing members are Brunei, Indonesia, Malaysia, the Philippines, Singapore, Thailand, and Vietnam. In addition, Burma and Laos were admitted to membership in July 1997.
2. See interview with Carl Greenidge, *The Courier*, No. 155, January–February 1996, p. 22.
3. See, for example, Robinson (1993), Sorenson (1993), Uvin (1993), Stokke (1995), Crawford (1995).
4. See Nelson and Eglinton (1992) p. 28 and Forsythe (1988) pp. 51–60. Nelson notes how, under Carter, 'For geopolitical reasons, human rights violations seemed to go unnoticed in The Philippines, South Korea, Iran (pre-1979), and Zaire'. Forsythe notes how 'the Reagan administration not only violated the law (Congressional human rights legislation) systematically but also said openly it was doing so' (pp. 51–2).
5. Beetham and Boyle (1995) p. 93.
6. Part II, paragraph 3, Final Declaration of the UN World Conference on Human Rights, Vienna, June 1993. It is noteworthy that these principles were initially stressed in the declarations from both the Latin American and Asia and Pacific Regional Preparatory meetings (UN 1993a).
7. A third policy instrument, not examined here, is the promotion of human rights and democracy through the provision of financial resources for project aid.
8. The European Council is the biannual summit meeting of Heads of Government, providing the general direction of policy development. Declarations were made at the Dublin Summit in June 1990 on human rights and good governance in Africa, at the Rome Summit in December 1990 on the promotion of democracy and human rights in external relations, and at the Luxembourg June 1991 Summit that respect for human rights, the rule of law and democratic political institutions are the basis for equitable development.
9. Part of the landmark nature of this Resolution was not only its content, but also it 'was the very first example of a joint resolution of the Council and Member States' (Chalker, 1992), signifying agreement on this common policy objective by all European Community members.
10. European Parliament (1991).
11. Article 130u, paragraph 2.
12. European Union (1991).
13. *Ibid.*
14. In legal terms, an essential element provides a firm legal basis for suspending the agreement in cases of serious and persistent human rights violations or interruptions of democratic processes. A suspension or non-performance clause establishes the specific rules agreed by the parties in such events. Without the latter, a party alleging breach of an essential element clause would seek recourse through the 1969 Vienna Convention on the Law of Treaties (Articles 60 & 65), involving a three-month delay and the opportunity for the other party to raise objections.

15.   De Feyter *et al.* (1995) p. 11.
16.   The few earlier references to human rights were restricted to the preamble of agreements, for example, in Lomé III.
17.   See Note 14.
18.   The most significant documents are: European Commission (1993); European Commission (1995a); European Commission (1995b); European Union (1995).
19.   European Commission (1995a).
20.   See Aelvoet Report (European Parliament, 1996).
21.   *Official Journal of the European Communities*, No. L 295/1990.
22.   *Official Journal of the European Communities*, No. L 79/1991.
23.   *Official Journal of the European Communities*, No. L 94/1992.
24.   *Official Journal of the European Communities*, No. L 313/1992.
25.   Pipkorn (1995) p. 40.
26.   Dates given in Napoli (undated), p. 13.
27.   *Official Journal of the European Communities*, No. L 403/1992.
28.   *Official Journal of the European Communities*, No. L 403/1992.
29.   *Official Journal of the European Communities*, No. L 189/1993.
30.   'Bulgarian' clause dates given in Napoli (undated), pp. 13–14.
31.   In addition, the MEDA Regulation, the financial mechanism of the new agreements, states that 'This Regulation is based on respect for democratic principles and the rule of law and also for human rights and fundamental freedoms, which constitute an essential element thereof, the violation of which element will justify the appropriate measures' (Article 3).
32.   European Commission (1993).
33.   European Commission (1995a) pp. 15–16.
34.   Stankovitch (1996) p. 7.
35.   European Commission (1994b).
36.   Ibid.
37.   European Commission (1995c) p. 7. This compares with a total of ECU 4.23 billion for the period 1978–91 (*ibid.*, p. 19).
38.   One could foresee the introduction of cosmetic changes, for example the release of a few political prisoners, as sufficient for the EU to state that there is a 'progressive trend' which they wish to encourage.
39.   Burma and Cuba are also included in Table 10.1 (making a total of 24 cases), both subject in different ways to EU pressure to implement political reforms.
40.   The EP's budgetary powers do not extend to aid under the Lomé Convention. This is not financed out of the general EU budget, but from the European Development Fund, raised separately by member states every five years.
41.   This excludes Burma where no agreement had been entered into.
42.   This excludes Nigeria where initial partial measures later became a total suspension of co-operation.
43.   It is possible there are more such cases, but by their nature they are less transparent to the researcher.
44.   See Note 3.
45.   Human Rights Watch (1992) p. 359.
46.   Amnesty International (1994a) p. 3.

47. US Department of State (1996) China Country Report, p. 2.
48. Member states are legally bound to implement CFSP 'Common positions', in contrast to the old-style 'declarations' or 'political statements' to which they are only honour bound. 'Common positions' are relatively few, however, with the large majority of CFSP activities remaining as 'Declarations'.
49. The *Guardian*, 21 July 1995 and 28 August 1995.
50. For example, the completion of a £150 million contract for 80 tanks, agreed in 1991 (*Guardian*, 28 August 1995).
51. The British government has not denied granting arms exports licences, but stated unconvincingly that they have not been for the supply of 'lethal defence equipment to the Nigerian armed forces', whilst refusing to reveal the details (*Guardian*, 28 August 1995).
52. US Department of State (1996) Overview, p. 4.
53. The *Guardian*, 21 November 1995.
54. Chalker (1995).
55. Human Rights Watch (1994) p. 244.
56. Resolution of the European Parliament 15 July 1993, '*La campagne de terrorisme menée par le PKK*'.
57. US Department of State (1995), *Press Briefing*, 1 February 1995, p. 17.
58. For example, External Affairs Commissioner Hans van den Broek stated that rejection of the customs union by the European Parliament could result in 'a severe backlash in Turkey' and that 'there is now every reason for the European Parliament to approve the accord' (cited in Human Rights Watch [1995] p. 244).
59. All aid statistics in these five country cases are taken from OECD (1996).
60. US Department of State (1996) *Indonesia Country Report*, pp. 1–2.
61. Human Rights Watch (1994) p. 157.
62. *Ibid.*, p. 158.
63. Instituto del Tercer Mundo (1995, p. 222) estimates 20 per cent and the World Development Movement (1996 election materials) states one-third.
64. Instituto del Tercer Mundo (1995) p. 222.
65. Amnesty International quoted the Sri Lankan government figure, that the JVP was responsible for over 6500 killings from late 1987 to March 1990, but retorted that the government themselves were responsible for 'disappearances and extrajudicial killings numbering tens of thousands (1991a, p. 209).
66. Human Rights Watch estimates '40 000 people disappeared between 1983 and 1992 after arrest by government forces or abduction by government-linked death squads' (1992, p. 186).
67. Human Rights Watch (1995) pp. 172–3.
68. *Ibid.*, p. 178.
69. For example, the targeting of relatives of known Islamists, particularly women, and generalised retaliatory actions against citizens in areas where armed groups are active Human Rights Watch (1994) pp. 256–9; Human Rights Watch (1995) pp. 263–6.
70. The cancellation of the elections brought no criticism from either the EU or from the Bush administration. The latter explicitly made clear its

preference for a military junta to a democratic process that resulted in a Islamic-dominated legislature. The EU's silence on human rights abuses and the democratic reversal is in marked contrast to their critical statements on events in many other countries.

71.   Human Rights Watch (1991) p. 630. Also see Amnesty International (1991b).
72.   Human Rights Watch (1995) p. 269.
73.   US Department of State (1996) *Egypt Country Report*, p. 1.
74.   US Department of State (1995) *Egypt Country Report*, p. 2.
75.   US Department of State (1995 & 1996), Human Rights Watch (1994) p. 264, and (1995) p. 270.
76.   The Andean Commission of Jurists – Colombian section has analyzed those cases where perpetrators are known. For the year until September 1992, it found that 40 per cent were attributable to state agents, 30 per cent to paramilitary groups, 27.5 per cent to guerillas, and 2.5 per cent to others including drug traffickers (Human Rights Watch [1992] p. 86). In 1995, 65 per cent were attributed to government security forces and 35 per cent to the guerillas (Human Rights Watch [1996] p. 79).
77.   Human Rights Watch (1995) p. 81.
78.   See Note 38.
79.   The Commission Unit is under-resourced, with a small, overworked staff. The EP subcommittee similarly relies on a small, overstretched staff, with its members' input limited by the restrictions on Parliament's powers. The intergovernmental mechanisms of the CFSP compare adversely in terms of resourcing with the equivalent sections of many member states' foreign ministries.
80.   Of particular relevance are the treaty-monitoring bodies of the UN human rights system, particularly the work of the Human Rights Committee and the Committee on Economic, Social and Cultural Rights, the supervisory bodies for the ICCPR and the ICESCR respectively. These examine the state party reports and submissions from other bodies, including NGOs, and produce their own reports and recommendations. In addition the reports of the UN Commission on Human Rights are of importance, though this body has the reputation of being more politicised.
81.   Van Boven (1995).
82.   Stokke (1995 pp. 56–62) discusses the prospects of an international regime administering political conditionality policies, and whilst not optimistic of its short-term realisation, similarly believes that it would be best situated within the United Nations. The DAC of the OECD may be an obvious choice of donors to perform such tasks, but a more genuinely international body, combining representatives from both North and South, would have greater legitimacy.
83.   See Vasco Ramos (1995), Deputy Director General, DGIA, European Commission.
84.   The division of competences and jurisdiction between the EU's institutional bodies is not entirely clear. Three procedures are outlined by a legal adviser of the Commission. First, the cancellation of an agreement is decided by the Council, following a proposal from the Commission and, depending on the case, after the assent of the EP. Second, the total suspen-

sion of an agreement follows the same procedure, except that, in the legal adviser's opinion, the assent of the EP is not required, only that they be informed. Third, partial suspension of co-operation remains the least clear. His opinion is that the Commission has the competence to do so: the power accorded to the Commission to execute a programme also extends to decision-making on measures partially to suspend programme activities (Pipkorn [1995] pp. 43–4).

References

Amnesty International (1990a) *Amnesty International Report 1989*. London: Amnesty International.

Amnesty International (1990b) *Sri Lanka: Extrajudicial executions, disappearances and torture 1987–90*. London: Amnesty International.

Amnesty International (1991a) *Amnesty International Report 1990*. London: Amnesty International.

Amnesty International (1991b) *Egypt: Ten Years of Torture*. London: Amnesty International.

Amnesty International (1994a) *Human Rights Violations Five Years After Tiananmen*. London: Amnesty International.

Amnesty International (1994b) *Colombia: Political Violence – Myth and Reality*. London: Amnesty International.

Barya, J.-J.B. (1993) 'The New Political Conditionalities of Aid: An Independent View From Africa', in IDS Bulletin.

Beetham, D. (1995) 'What Future for Economic and Social Rights?', in *Political Studies* XLIII.

Beetham, D. and Boyle, K. (1995) *Introducing Democracy: Eighty Questions and Answers*. Paris: UNESCO.

Chalker, L. (1991) 'Good Government and the Aid Programme', transcript of speech at the Royal Institute of International Affairs, 25 July 1991. London: Overseas Development Administration.

Chalker, L. (1992) 'Priorities in Development for the European Community', transcript of speech to the All Party Parliamentary Group on Overseas Development, 25 November 1992. London: Overseas Development Administration.

Chalker, L. (1994) 'Good Government: Putting Policy into Practice', transcript of speech to the Royal Institute of International Affairs, 6 July 1994, London: ODA.

Chalker, L. (1995) transcript of speech at House of Lords debate on Nigeria, 7 March 1995.

Courier, The (July–August 1991) 'Human Rights, Democracy and Development', No. 128. Brussels: European Commission.

Courier, The (May–June 1993) 'ACP–EC Joint Assembly in Gaborone', No. 139. Brussels: European Commission.

Courier, The (January–February 1996) No. 155. Brussels: European Commission.

Crawford, G. (1995) *Promoting Democracy, Human Rights and Good Govern-ance Development Aid: A Comparative Study of the Policies of Four Northern Donors*. University of Leeds: Centre for Democratization Studies.

De Feyter, K. *et al.* (1995) *Development Co-operation: a tool for the promotion of human rights and democratization*. Brussels: Belgian Ministry for Develop-ment Co-operation.

Euro-Cidse (1993) *News Bulletin*, September 1993 and November–December 1993. Brussels: Euro-Cidse.

European Commission (1991) *Communication to the Council and Parliament on 'Human Rights, Democracy and Development'*, 25 March 1991. Doc. No. SEC(91) 61. Brussels: European Commission.

European Commission (1992) *Report on the Implementation of the Resolution of the Council on Human Rights, Democracy and Development adopted on 28 No-vember 1991*. Doc. No. SEC (92) 1915, 21 October 1992. Brussels: European Commission.

European Commission (1993) Communication from the President and the Commissioner for External Relations to the Commission *Sur la prise en compte des droits de l'homme et des valeurs démocratiques dans les accords entre la Communauté et les pays tiers*. Doc. No. SEC (93) 50/4, 22 January 1993. Brus-sels: European Commission.

European Commission (1994a) *Report on the Implementation in 1993 of the Reso-lution of the Council on Human rights, Democracy and Development adopted on 28 November 1991*. Doc. No. COM (94) 42, 23 February 1994. Brussels: Euro-pean Commission.

European Commission (1994b) *Towards a New Asia Strategy*, Communication to the Council. Doc. No. COM (94) 314, 13 July 1994. Brussels: European Com-mission.

European Commission (1994c) *Memorandum on the Community's Development Aid in 1993* (to the Development Assistance Committee). Brussels: European Commission.

European Commission (1995a) Communication *On the Inclusion of Respect for Democratic Principles and Human Rights in Agreements between the Commun-ity and Third Countries* Doc. No. COM (95) 216, 23 May 1995. Brussels: Euro-pean Commission.

European Commission (1995b) Communication to the Council and Parliament on *The European Union and the External Dimension of Human Rights Policy: From Rome to Maastricht and Beyond*. Doc. No. COM (95) 567, 22 November 1995. Brussels: European Commission.

European Commission (1995c) *Memorandum on the Community's Development Aid in 1994* (to the Development Assistance Committee). Brussels: European Commission.

European Commission (1996) *Report on the Implementation in 1994 of the Resolu-tion of the Council on Human rights, Democracy and Development adopted on 28 November 1991*. Doc. No. VIII/1406/95 – EN. Brussels: European Commission.

European Parliament (1991) *Resolution on human rights and development policy*, adopted 22 November 1991. Doc. No. PE 155.084. Luxembourg: European Parliament.

European Parliament (1993) *Suivi des Résolutions D'Initiative Adoptées par le Parlement Européen de Juillet 1989 à Juillet 1993*. Document de Travail.

European Parliament (1995a) *Report on human rights in the world in 1993–94 and the Union's human rights policy* (Imbeni Report). Doc. No. PE 211.973. Luxembourg: European Parliament.

European Parliament (1995b) *Human Rights Clause in External Agreements*, Summary record of presentations made at the Public Hearing, 20–21 November 1995. Luxembourg: European Parliament.

European Parliament (1996), *Report on human rights clauses in EU agreements with third countries* (Aelvoet Report, Committee on Development and Co-operation, February 1996). Luxembourg: European Parliament.

European Union Council of Ministers (Development) (1991) *Resolution of the Council and of the Member States meeting in the Council on Human Rights, Democracy and Development*, 28 November 1991. Doc. No. 10 107/91. Brussels: European Commission.

European Union Council of Ministers (Development) (1993) *Declaration on Human Rights, Democracy and Development*, 25 May 1993. Doc. No. 6705/93. Brussels: European Commission.

European Union Council of Ministers (General Affairs) (1995) 29 May 1995. Doc. No. 7255/95. Brussels: European Commission.

Forsythe, D.P. (1988) *Human Rights and US Foreign Policy: Congress Reconsidered* Gainesville: University of Florida Press.

Human Rights Watch (1990) *Human Rights Watch World Report 1991: Events of 1990*. New York: Human Rights Watch.

Human Rights Watch (1991) *Human Rights Watch World Report 1992: Events of 1991*. New York: Human Rights Watch.

Human Rights Watch (1992) *Human Rights Watch World Report 1993: Events of 1992*. New York: Human Rights Watch.

Human Rights Watch (1993) *Human Rights Watch World Report 1994: Events of 1993*. New York: Human Rights Watch.

Human Rights Watch (1994) *Human Rights Watch World Report 1995: Events of 1994*. New York: Human Rights Watch.

Human Rights Watch (1995) *Human Rights Watch World Report 1996: Events of 1995*. New York: Human Rights Watch.

IDS Bulletin Vol. 24 No. 1 (January 1993) *Good Government*. Brighton: Institute of Development Studies.

Instituto del Tercer Mundo (1995) *The World: A Third World Guide 1995/96*. Montevideo: Instituto del Tercer Mundo.

Muzaffar, C. (1995) 'EU policy: a perspective from Asia', in European Parliament (1995b).

Napoli, D. (undated) *Elements d'une Politique Externe de l'Union Européenne en Matiere deDroits de l'Homme* (mimeo).

Nelson, J. and Eglinton, S.J. (1992) *Encouraging Democracy: What Role for Conditioned Aid?* Washington DC: Overseas Development Council.

OECD (1996) *Geographical Distribution of Financial Flows to Aid Recipients 1990–94*, Paris: Development Assistance Committee/OECD.

Official Journal of the European Communities (various editions). Brussels and Luxemburg: Official Office for Publications of the European Union.

Pipkorn, J. (1995) 'Legal aspects of the application of the human rights clause', in European Parliament (1995b).

Ramos, V. (1995) 'Outline of the EU's policy objectives', in European Parliament (1995b).

Robinson, K. (1993) 'Will Political Conditionality Work?' in *IDS Bulletin*.

Sorenson, G. (ed.) (1993) *Political Conditionality*. London: Frank Cass/EADI.

Stankovitch, M. (1996) *The European Union and ASEAN – a background paper*. London: Catholic Institute for International Relations.

Stokke, O. (ed.) (1995) *Aid and Political Conditionality*. London: Frank Cass/EADI.

United Nations (1993a) *World Conference on Human Rights, Vienna, Austria, June 1993: Information Pack*. New York: UN.

United Nations (1993b) *Vienna Declaration and Programme of Action, 25 June 1993*. New York: UN.

United States Department of State (1995) *Country Reports on Human Rights Practices for 1994*. Washington D.C.: US Department of State.

United States Department of State (1996) *Country Reports on Human Rights Practices for 1995*. Washington D.C.: US Department of State.

Uvin. P. (1993) 'Do as I say, Not as I do: The Limits of Political Conditionality', in Sorenson (1993).

van Boven, T. (1995) 'The international legal context of the EU's evolving policy', in European Parliament (1995b).

Index

Note: 'n.' after a page reference incicates the number of a note on that page.

179